Relish MIDLANDS

Original recipes from the region's best-loved chefs and restaurants. Introduction by chef patron Glynn Purnell.

First Published 2019
By Relish Publications
Morpeth, Northumberland, NE61 1PY

Twitter: @Relish_Cookbook
Facebook: RelishRestaurantGuide
Instagram: Relish_Cookbook
For cookbooks and recipes visit:
www.relishpublications.co.uk

ISBN: 978-0-9934678-9-9

Publisher: Duncan L Peters
General Manager: Teresa Peters
Design: Vicki Brown
Proofing Coordinator: Valerie McLeod
Relish Photography: Michelle Martin, Visual
Voice Media
Special Thanks: Andy Richardson, Away With Media

Front cover photograph by: Michelle Martin,
Visual Voice Media

Printed in Poland on behalf of Latitude Press.

Welcome to this third edition of Relish Midlands, with a mouthwatering selection of recipes from the region's best-loved chefs and restaurants. We know you will enjoy visiting or cooking your way through the pages of this carefully curated collection.

Relish Publications began life in 2009 when two food lovers and experienced publishers (Duncan and Teresa) unfolded a new concept in recipe books, which reflect the same attention to detail and care that our featured chefs deliver, each and every day.

We have circumnavigated the UK in our hunt for the most highly acclaimed eateries, hidden gems and those highly recommended by other best-loved chefs in the UK.

We invite you to join our Relish community on Instagram, Facebook and Twitter. We love to hear from our readers and so do the Relish chefs.

Best wishes,

Duncan and Teresa Peters

004
CONTENTS

006
CONTENTS

Salad of Crab, Wasabi Crème Fraîche, Pickled Cucumber, Radish - **Page 120**

009
STARTERS

011
MAINS

Iced Vanilla Parfait, Rhubarb Textures, Oat Crumble, Rhubarb Sorbet - **Page 134**

013
DESSERTS

015
FOREWORD BY GLYNN PURNELL

"Birmingham. The centre of the universe. At least that's what I reckon. And I should know. I've travelled and worked all around the world but there's no place like home.

When I won a Michelin star in 2005, I achieved all my dreams. I'd grown up on a council estate, in Chelmsley Wood, and all I'd ever wanted to do was cook. I blagged my way into my first job at the Metropole Hotel, in Birmingham, when I was supposed to be doing work experience at the NEC and I've never looked back.

Food is all about emotion, about memory, about transporting people in the way that great music or films might. And that's what we like to do at Purnell's. It's what so many of my fellow chefs across the Midlands also do.

And so I'm delighted to kick off the new edition of Relish Midlands by contributing a foreword and welcoming you, the reader, on board.

We have some fantastic restaurants across the region, a number of sensational producers and some supremely talented restaurateurs. Birmingham has more Michelin stars than anywhere in the UK outside London - but the 'second city' is about more than just that. It's about passion and industry, hard work and skill, talent and vision. And, in this third edition of Relish Midlands, the crème de la crème show what they're made of.

In the Midlands, we're used to turning things to our advantage. So although we're landlocked, we make the most of transport links with fishermen ferrying day boat fish from Scotland, Devon or Cornwall. We have brilliant farmers and growers, people who are experts in their field. And that's what local restaurateurs bring to the table as they prepare food with guile and craft.

Birmingham's reputation has spread around the world - it's not so long ago that the New York Times was praising our food and drink credentials - and our surrounding counties are equally noteworthy.

So I hope you use the latest instalment of Relish as a guide to restaurants worth checking out. I've been flying the flag for Birmingham for a few decades now - so come on down, make the trip, you'll be stunned by what's on offer."

Glynn Purnell
Chef Patron, Purnell's

016
ADAM'S

New Oxford House, 16 Waterloo Street, Birmingham, B2 5UG

0121 643 3745
www.adamsrestaurant.co.uk Twitter: @RestaurantAdams

A dam's was opened in 2013, by husband and wife team Adam and Natasha, in a former sandwich shop. Intended as a two year 'pop-up', the couple continued to look for a location for the restaurant's permanent home. Patience paid off when, in summer 2015, they took on three floors of New Oxford House on Waterloo Street. After a complete renovation the restaurant was able to move into its new location in January 2016.

The 36-cover dining room serves a three course menu, alongside the signature tasting menu and a weekday lunch menu. A private dining room adjacent to the main dining room is available for up to 17 guests. Downstairs in the kitchen, guests can dine at the Chef's Table and view the equally impressive wine room.

The aim is to create a unique experience for each diner, informal yet elegant. Adam's has become a landmark venue within the gastronomic landscape of Birmingham and the Midlands, serving modern British food in a comfortable and relaxed setting.

Owner Adam Stokes heads up the award-winning restaurant, supported by head chef Tom Shepherd, holding a string of accolades including a Michelin star, three AA Rosettes and a score of '7' in the Good Food Guide.

Modern and stylish Michelin-starred cooking in the centre of Birmingham, with an emphasis on flavour, in a relaxed environment.

COD, MUSSELS, CHAMPAGNE

SERVES 4

🍷 *2016 Sancerre 'Garennes' Domaine Laporte 2016, Loire Valley (France)*

Ingredients

Cod

1 cod loin
seasoning

Mussel Velouté

1kg mussels
1 bottle Champagne
2 shallots (chopped)
2 cloves garlic (chopped)
250ml whipping cream

Confit Lemon Purée

12 lemons
150g sugar
150ml water

Potato Purée

4 Désirée potatoes
100ml double cream
100g butter
150ml whole milk

Vegetables

1 kohlrabi
sea aster

To Serve

dill oil
smoked caviar

Method

For The Cod

Season the cod lightly and roll tightly in cling film. Place in the fridge until cooking, this will help shape the cod. Just before cooking, take out of the fridge and cook *sous vide* at 50°C for 12-14 minutes, depending on the thickness.

For The Mussel Velouté

Rinse the mussels in clean, cold water for around 30 minutes. Place a large pan on the stove and turn the heat up to full. Place the mussels, along with the Champagne, in the pan and pop a lid on. Wait until all the mussels have opened (around 1-2 minutes), then strain through a sieve. Place the mussels in the fridge and reserve the cooking liquid for the velouté.

Lightly fry the shallots and garlic in a pan, then add the cooking liquid and reduce to a glaze. Pour in the cream and bring back to the boil. Taste for seasoning, then pass through a sieve and chill. To serve, gently reheat the mussels in the sauce.

> **Chef's Tip**
>
> Ensure your mussels are as fresh as possible, so all should be closed, clean and smell of the sea. With this, your sauce will be delicious.

For The Confit Lemon Purée

Peel the lemons and place the rind in cold water, bring to the boil, then pass the liquid off. Repeat the process 3 more times, saving the water from the second boil. In a separate pan, place the sugar, water and 150ml of the reserved lemon water and bring to the boil. Add the rind and gently simmer for 1 hour. Blend, then refrigerate until set. Pipe a small amount on top of the cooked fish.

For The Potato Purée

Preheat the oven to 160°C.

Bake the potatoes for 1 hour, allow to cool, then scoop out the flesh. Bring the cream, butter and milk to the boil, then add the potato flesh and mash until smooth. Season with salt.

For The Vegetables

We use a spiraliser for a twist on the kohlrabi so, if like us, you have a spiraliser, spiralise the kohlrabi and boil until cooked just before serving.

Simply wash the sea aster and keep in the fridge. To cook, treat exactly like spinach.

To Serve

Portion the cod into 4 and serve as pictured.

PORK PRESA, MORELS, SWEDE, WILD GARLIC

SERVES 4

 Batuta, Niepoort, Douro, 2003 (Portugal)

Ingredients

Pork

750g piece Iberico pork presa
500g pork belly
250g mixed vegetables (carrots, onions) (chopped)
150ml chicken stock

Wild Garlic And Oil

500g wild garlic
100ml oil
salt (pinch of)

Morels

100g morels
butter (large knob of)

Swede

1 whole swede
oil (for frying)

Hollandaise

1 shallot (chopped)
100ml white wine
100ml white wine vinegar
2 egg yolks
200g *clarified butter*
salt (pinch of)
lemon juice (spritz of)

Method

For The Pork Presa

Season the presa lightly. Heat a frying pan until red hot and fry the presa as you would a steak. We prefer to cook medium at Adam's, but equally it eats well at whatever degree you prefer. We cook for around 3-4 minutes a side and rest for 8 minutes.

Chef's Tip

Ensure the pork presa is at room temperature before cooking, equally rest the presa for the same amount of time you cooked it.

For The Pork Belly

Preheat the oven to 130°C.

Season the belly and place in an oven tray on top of the mixed vegetables. Pour in the stock and cover with foil. Cook for 3 hours. Just before serving, turn the oven up to 220°C, remove the foil and cook for a further 20 minutes to crisp the skin. Cut and serve.

For The Wild Garlic And Oil

To make the oil, blend 450g of the garlic with the oil and salt. Blend to a smooth pesto, then pass through a sieve to extract the oil.

Bring a pan of water to the boil, then place the remaining wild garlic in the water for 30 seconds. Season and serve.

For The Morels

Simply cook the morels for 2 minutes in foaming butter.

For The Swede

Preheat the oven to 160°C.

Bake the swede whole for 2 hours. Allow to cool, then, using a corer, cut to desired shape.

With the remainder of the swede, make a crumble by chopping the leftovers and deep frying until golden brown (180°C). Season, then roll the shaped swede through the crumb for texture.

For The Hollandaise

Place the shallot, wine and vinegar in a pan and reduce to a glaze. Allow to cool to room temperature.

In the same pan, whisk the yolks over a very low heat until the volume doubles. Slowly pour in the *clarified butter*, continually whisking. Once thickened, season with salt and lemon juice.

To Serve

Serve as pictured.

GATEAU OPERA, PEANUT, CARAMEL, TERIYAKI

SERVES 4

🍷 *Trockenbeerenauslese No 6, Weinlaubenhof
Kracher, 2007, Burgenland (Austria)*

Ingredients

Gâteau Opéra Sponge

3 large eggs
125g icing sugar
40g plain flour
11g cocoa powder
125g peanut butter
30g butter (melted)

Peanut Mousse

200ml double cream
100ml whole milk
50g peanut butter
1½ leaves gelatine (soaked in cold water)
120g milk chocolate

Teriyaki Caramel Buttercream

220g sugar
100ml double cream
30g teriyaki sauce
70g butter

To Serve (Optional)

peanut ice cream
chocolate marquise
peanut brittle
tempered chocolate

Method

> **Chef's Tip**
>
> When making the opéra, it's good to make it the night before you serve, allowing time to press so your lines are sharp.

For The Gâteau Opéra Sponge

Preheat the oven to 160°C.

Whisk the eggs until doubled in volume. Slowly incorporate all the dry ingredients, then mix in the peanut butter and add the melted butter at the end. Spread the mix about a £1 coin thickness on greaseproof paper and transfer to a large, flat tray. Bake for 6 minutes. Once cooked, allow to cool completely and cut into 5 even-sized pieces.

For The Peanut Mousse

Heat the cream, milk and peanut butter in a pan and boil. Once boiled, stir in the gelatine, then pour over the chocolate and allow it to melt for 5 minutes. Blend with a stick blender until smooth, then transfer to the fridge to set.

For The Teriyaki Caramel Buttercream

Make a caramel with the sugar, then add the cream and teriyaki sauce. Bring to the boil, then slowly whisk in the butter. Once incorporated, transfer to the fridge to set.

To Build The Opéra

Place the sheets of cooled sponge on a clean open workbench and spread a thin layer, around a £1 coin thickness, of peanut mousse on one, ensuring it goes right to the edge. Place another sheet of sponge on top and repeat with the teriyaki caramel. Repeat this double process again so you have 4 layers of filling and 5 sheets of sponge. Gently place on a flat tray, with a piece of greaseproof paper on the top and bottom. Place a light weight on top of the opéra and leave in the fridge to press overnight.

Slice to your desired thickness and allow to come up to room temperature before serving.

To Serve

We serve the gateau opéra with a *quenelle* of peanut ice cream and chocolate marquise, peanut brittle and tempered chocolate.

THE BAITING HOUSE

Upper Sapey, Worcestershire, WR6 6XT

01886 853 201
www.baitinghouse.co.uk Instagram: The Baiting House Facebook: The Baiting House

A t the top of the hill climbing out of the Teme Valley, just as you cross the border from Worcestershire into Herefordshire, lies the small village of Upper Sapey. The focal point of village life for well over a century, The Baiting House was traditionally where drovers and waggoners climbing the hill with their horses would stop for 'bait' (the local word for food, or a small snack).

Since a complete refurbishment under the ownership of local couple Kate Lane and Andrew Cornthwaite, The Baiting House has firmly established itself as a favourite for local foodies. This award-winning inn welcomes guests from all over the world, who come to sample the bold, modern cooking, followed by a night in one of the six lovely bedrooms, or in the luxury wooden cabins scattered throughout the five-acre grounds.

Head chef Charles Bradley, who previously trained at the Michelin star restaurant Mr Underhills of Ludlow, has been at The Baiting House since day one and, together with a small team of chefs, offers a daily changing menu that has brought recognition from the Good Food Guide, Hardens Guide and the AA.

As well as the AA 2 Rosette à la carte menu, The Baiting House offers a well-chosen wine list, as well as an excellent selection of local cask ales and ciders from local producers.

Modern British cooking; bold flavours with an emphasis on locally sourced produce. The Baiting House also offers six en-suite bedrooms and five luxury lodges.

BEETROOT CURED SALMON, HORSERADISH, DILL, NEW POTATO, CUCUMBER

SERVES 4

 Grüner Veltliner Weingut Rabl, 2017 (Austria)

Ingredients

Beetroot Cured Salmon

500g raw beetroot (peeled)
3g fennel seeds
½ bunch tarragon
250g caster sugar
500g sea salt
½ side of salmon

Horseradish Cream

150ml whipping cream
1 tsp Dijon mustard
fresh horseradish (knob of, peeled, finely grated)
sea salt flakes

Compressed Cucumber

½ tsp salt
1 tbsp honey
3 tbsp rapeseed oil
1 cucumber (peeled, deseeded)

Dill Oil

100g dill (picked)
100ml olive pomace oil

To Serve

4 new potatoes (boiled, cooled, sliced)
caviar
dill (picked)
chervil (picked)
red onion (sliced)

Method

For The Beetroot Cured Salmon (Prepare ahead)

Dice the beetroot into 3cm cubes, then blend with the fennel seeds, tarragon, sugar and sea salt, in a food processor, to make the cure.

Pin bone and trim the salmon. Lay it on a large tray and pour the cure over. Cover with cling film, then leave in the fridge for 10 hours. Turn the salmon over and cure for another 10 hours. Tip away the juices, wash off the cure and pat the salmon dry.

Chef's Tip

Source wild salmon, if possible, for a better flavour.

For The Horseradish Cream

Place the whipping cream and mustard in a bowl and whisk together to form soft peaks. Carefully fold in the grated horseradish. Season with salt.

For The Compressed Cucumber

Mix the salt, honey and oil together. Scoop the cucumber into balls and put in a vac pack bag with the dressing and seal. Leave to compress for at least 1 hour.

For The Dill Oil

Blanch the dill in boiling, salted water for 30 seconds, then refresh in iced water and squeeze out the excess water. Blitz with the oil, then strain through muslin cloth.

To Serve

Slice the salmon allowing 2 slices per portion. Arrange the compressed cucumber, potato and horseradish cream on top and around the salmon. Add the caviar and picked herbs, and finish with the dill oil.

RUMP OF LAMB, POTATO & TURNIP GRATIN, ONION, BABY LEEKS, LAMB SAUCE

SERVES 4

Châteauneuf-du-Pape, Château Fortia 2013
(France)

Ingredients

Lamb Rump
4 x 225g lamb rumps
4 sprigs fresh thyme
4 sprigs fresh rosemary
olive oil (drizzle of)

Onion Purée
3 large sweet onions (finely sliced)
oil (dash of)
1 clove garlic (finely sliced)
1 sprig fresh thyme
250ml double cream
50g butter
salt and white pepper

Potato And Turnip Gratin
600g Maris Piper potatoes (peeled)
600g turnips
600ml double cream
3 cloves garlic (grated)
ground white pepper
butter (large knob of)

Baby Leeks
8 baby leeks (trimmed, washed)

Lamb Sauce
100g butter
1½kg lamb bones (finely chopped)
1½kg lamb fat (finely diced)
1½ litres chicken stock (hot)

Garnish
charred onion petals
baby spinach leaves

large gratin dish (greased)

Method

For The Lamb Rump
Trim off the fat and score the flesh. Seal in a vac pack bag with the olive oil, thyme and rosemary. Cook in a water bath for 45 minutes at 58½°C. Remove the lamb, pat dry and colour, skin-side down, in a hot pan. Alternatively, roast the lamb (180°C fan) for 12-15 minutes until the core temperature reaches 55°C. Leave to rest.

For The Onion Purée
Sweat the onions down in a pan in a little oil until cooked and caramelised. Add the garlic and thyme and cook until the garlic is tender. Stir in the cream and butter. Remove the thyme before blitzing in a blender, then pass through a fine sieve. Season to taste.

For The Potato And Turnip Gratin
Preheat the oven to 150°C (fan).

Slice the potatoes and turnips about 2mm thick, then toss together in a large bowl.

Add the cream, garlic, salt and some white pepper to a pan and bring to the boil.

Layer the potatoes and turnips in the prepared gratin dish, slightly overlapping each other. Pour over the warm cream and bake for 1 hour. Leave to cool slightly.

For The Baby Leeks
Blanch in boiling salted water, refresh in iced water until needed.

For The Lamb Sauce
Heat the butter in a pan, add the lamb bones and fat, cook until golden brown. Cover with the hot stock. Bring to the boil, skim, then reduce to your desired consistency. Strain into a clean pan.

To Serve
Swirl the onion purée onto a plate. Add a spoonful of turnip gratin and 2 slices of carved lamb. Top with baby leeks, spinach, onion petals, then spoon over the lamb sauce.

Chef's Tip
The sauce and vegetables can be prepared in advance and simply reheated when serving.

LEMON POSSET, LEMON FINANCIER, RASPBERRY SORBET, HONEYCOMB

SERVES 4

🍷 *Moscato d'Asti Michele Chiarlo 2017 (Italy)*

Ingredients

Lemon Posset

125g caster sugar
450ml double cream
1 lemon (zest of)
60ml lemon juice

Lemon Financier

55g unsalted butter (plus extra for greasing)
2 lemons (zest of)
22g plain flour
20g ground almonds
40g icing sugar
40g egg white (room temperature)

Raspberry Sorbet

120g caster sugar
50ml water
1kg raspberry purée

Honeycomb

200g caster sugar
60g golden syrup
200ml glucose syrup
20g bicarbonate of soda

4 glasses or jars
non-stick mini muffin mould (greased)
large tray (lined)

Method

For The Lemon Posset

Add the sugar, cream and zest to a pan and gently heat to melt the sugar. Add the lemon juice and boil for 2 minutes. Pour into individual serving glasses or jars, cover and leave to set in the fridge for 3-4 hours.

> **Chef's Tip**
> Make the lemon possets a day before for a better set.

For The Lemon Financier

Add the butter to a small pan and heat gently until it starts to turn a golden brown colour. As soon as it does, remove from the heat and set aside. Mix together the dry ingredients and stir in the egg whites. Stir in the butter until a smooth. Refrigerate for 2 hours.

Preheat the oven to 200°C (fan).

Spoon the batter into the muffin moulds, filling to three-quarters full. Bake for 8-10 minutes until golden, leave to cool.

For The Raspberry Sorbet

Boil the sugar and water, then remove from the heat and allow to cool. Once cool, stir the raspberry purée into the syrup until combined. Churn in an ice cream machine until frozen.

For The Honeycomb

Add the sugar, golden syrup and glucose to a pan. Place the pan over a medium heat and heat to a light golden brown caramel. The temperature should reach 165°C on a sugar thermometer. Sprinkle the bicarbonate of soda on and stir through. Pour onto the lined tray. Leave to cool for 20 minutes, or until it has set firm. Break into small pieces.

To Serve

Arrange the posset, financier and sorbet on a plate. Top each posset with honeycomb.

036
THE BELFRY HOTEL & RESORT, RYDER GRILL

Lichfield Road, Sutton Coldfield, B76 9PR

01675 238 600
www.thebelfry.com Twitter: @thebelfryhotel Instagram: @thebelfryhotelandresort
Facebook: @BelfryHotel

Executive head chef Robert Bates joined The Belfry in 2013, having previously worked in several Michelin star restaurants and hotels around the UK and Europe, bringing with him a wealth of skills and culinary experiences.

Exquisite dining is a staple of The Belfry, with gastronomic excellence on offer at their signature restaurant; The Ryder Grill, serving up an à la carte menu made up of succulent steaks, chargrills, fish and lobster. The à la carte experience is cooked fresh to order, served exactly as guests want it, with the menu providing a refreshing take on modern dining.

Having been named England's Leading Resort at The World Travel Awards for three consecutive years, achieving the TripAdvisor Certificate of Excellence and an AA Rosette, The Belfry and The Ryder Grill have developed a name for excellence in the hospitality industry, attracting visitors from all over the world.

Set against the backdrop of 550 acres of North Warwickshire countryside, yet just 20 minutes outside of Birmingham City Centre, The Belfry has three golf courses, luxurious guest bedrooms and suites, an award-winning club house, meeting and events rooms, restaurants and bars, as well as a spa and leisure club.

As winner of the prestigious 'Hotel Chef of the Year', executive head chef Robert Bates and his team deliver a first-class culinary experience for each and every guest who visits The Belfry.

SESAME GLAZED CONFIT DUCK LEG PASTILLA, SWEET & SOUR SPICED PLUMS, PARSNIP PUREE

SERVES 4

 Ara, Sauvignon Blanc (New Zealand)
This wine works well with the sweet and sour
elements to this dish.

Ingredients

Duck Leg Confit And Pastilla

Step 1:
2 large duck legs
25g sea salt
thyme (pinch of)
800g duck fat

Step 2:
75g hoisin sauce
75g red wine jus
25g spring onion (*julienne*)

Step 3:
1 sheet brick pastry
oil (for deep frying)
icing sugar (to dust)
piment espelette
sesame seeds

Sweet And Sour Spiced Plums

50g Demerara sugar
250ml red wine
½ stick cinnamon
2g ginger
five spice (pinch of)
200g plums (halved)

Parsnip Purée

400g medium-sized parsnips (peeled)
200ml whole milk
150ml double cream
30g butter
thyme (pinch of)
salt (to taste)

Garnish

baby gem lettuce, micro coriander

Method

For The Duck Leg Confit And Pastilla (Prepare ahead)

Trim the duck legs of excess fat, then sprinkle both sides with sea salt and thyme. Leave for 2-3 hours, then brush the excess salt off.

Preheat the oven to 130°C (fan).

Place the legs in a deep tray, cover with duck fat and cook in the oven for 3 hours until tender; the fat should not 'boil'. Leave to cool in the fat. When cool, pick the meat from the legs and place into a container. Add the ingredients from Step 2 and combine well.

Divide the mix into 4 and wrap each amount of the mixture tightly in the brick pastry to form cigar shapes. Set aside.

> **Chef's Tip**
>
> Roll the pastilla tight to avoid air holes, so it cooks evenly and stays crispy.

For The Sweet And Sour Spiced Plums

Combine all the ingredients, except the plums, in a pan and reduce by half to a syrupy consistency. Add the plums, cover with cling film and allow to cool.

For The Parsnip Purée

Cut the parsnips into 2cm dice. Place in a saucepan with the other ingredients, cover with a *cartouche* and bring to a simmer. Cook gently until the parsnips are very soft. Drain the liquid and set aside. Blitz the parsnips in a blender for 2-3 minutes until very smooth, adding some of the liquid if necessary. Season to taste.

To Serve

Preheat the oven to 180°C (fan).

Deep fry (180°C) the pastilla until crispy, about 2-3 minutes. Place into the oven for 2 minutes, then dust with icing sugar, piment espelette and sprinkle with sesame seeds. Cut into 3. Serve as pictured, garnished with baby gem and micro coriander.

OX CHEEK, KIBBLED ONION CRUMB, PICKLED ONION RINGS, SPINACH PUREE, RED WINE JUS

SERVES 4

🍷 *Catena, Malbec (Argentina)*
A good full-bodied red wine to accompany this dish. Chef Bates personal favourite!

Ingredients

Braised Ox Cheeks

1.4kg ox cheek (untrimmed)
160g carrots (chopped)
160g onions (chopped)
100g celery (chopped)
20g garlic (chopped)
10g thyme sprigs, 900ml red wine
40ml vegetable oil, 50g tomato paste
1 litre veal stock, 10g salt, 2g pepper

Kibbled Onion Crumb

75g panko breadcrumbs
25g kibbled onions
5g flat leaf parsley (finely chopped)
3g Maldon sea salt

Pickled Onion Rings

100ml cider vinegar
50g sugar, thyme (pinch of)
100g grelot onions (whole weight) (sliced)

Spinach Purée

25g shallots (chopped)
5g garlic (puréed)
60g butter
300g spinach
100ml double cream
salt (to taste), ice (to chill)

Mashed Potatoes

300g Red Rooster potatoes
100g cold butter (diced)
20ml double cream (warmed)
salt (to taste)

To Serve

heritage carrots

Method

For The Braised Ox Cheeks (Prepare ahead, allow 48 hours)

Trim and clean the meat. Place the cheeks in cold running water for around 10-15 minutes. Drain well, then place the beef in a non-reactive container with the *mirepoix*, garlic and thyme. Cover with the wine and leave to marinate overnight.

Drain the meat and *mirepoix*. Heat up the oil to very hot and seal the meat until caramelised on all surfaces. Remove the meat, reduce the heat and *sauté* the *mirepoix* until golden brown. Add the tomato paste and cook for 10 minutes. Add the wine and return the meat to the pan. Simmer for 5 minutes. Add the stock and seasoning, bring to a simmer and skim the surface. Reduce the heat, cook until tender overnight at 85°C, or for around 10-12 hours. Remove from the heat and leave to cool for 1 hour. Remove the meat from the sauce and chill. Strain the sauce and reduce if necessary. Check seasoning and chill.

For The Kibbled Onion Crumb

Lightly toast the breadcrumbs, then allow to cool. Combine with the other ingredients.

For The Pickled Onion Rings

Bring the vinegar, sugar and thyme to the boil. Add the sliced onions, cover with cling film and leave to cool.

For The Spinach Purée

Sweat the shallots and garlic in the butter until soft, then add the spinach leaves. Pour in the cream, bring to the boil and cook for 4 minutes until the cream has reduced by half. Transfer to a blender and blitz well. Season, then pass through a sieve into a bowl set over ice to retain the colour.

For The Mashed Potatoes

Cook the potatoes in slightly salted water. When fully cooked, drain from the water, then leave to dry out for a few minutes. While still hot, mix in the hard butter, the warm double cream and salt.

To Serve

Gently reheat the ox cheek in the red wine jus. Place the onion crumb on top, pipe the mashed potatoes onto the plate and served as pictured.

Chef's Tip

It is very important to make sure the braised ox cheek is gently reheated and basted until nice and sticky.

DARK CHOCOLATE DELICE, TROPICAL FRUITS, CASHEW NUTS

SERVES 12

🍷 *Royal Tokaji Late Harvest (Hungary)*
This wine goes great with the tropical flavours of this dish.

Ingredients

Chocolate Sponge

60g egg yolk, 60g caster sugar
12g flour (sifted), 12g cornflour (sifted)
14g cocoa powder (sifted), 2 egg whites (65g)
28g butter (melted)

Crispy Base

56g dark chocolate (70%)
140g cashew praline paste
100g feuilletine or corn flakes, 150g Nutella

Chocolate Mousse

700ml whipping cream
3 egg yolks (60g), 44g caster sugar
330g dark chocolate (54%) (chopped)

Coconut Jelly

250ml coconut milk
1 lime (juice and zest of), 50g caster sugar
2½g gelatine (soaked in cold water)

Coconut Oil Glaze/Spray

140g dark chocolate (70%), 60g coconut oil

Pineapple And Passion Fruit Sorbet

125g caster sugar, 125ml water
200g fresh pineapple (chopped)
150ml passion fruit purée

Garnish

sugared cashew nuts, mango cream

36cm x 16cm tray (lined with cling film)
36cm x 16cm metal frame

Chef's Tip

You must make this dessert in advance so it's ideal for a dinner party. Save the leftover sponge in the freezer for use in other desserts.

Method

For The Chocolate Sponge

Preheat the oven to 180°C (fan).
Beat together the yolks and half the sugar. Combine the flour, cornflour and cocoa. Whisk the egg whites with the remaining sugar. Add the dry ingredients to the beaten yolks and sugar, fold in the meringue, then the melted butter. Spread onto baking paper, 1cm high, and bake until cooked, about 5 minutes. Leave to cool. Cut to a rectangle, 36cm x 16cm.

For The Crispy Base

Melt the chocolate gently in a microwave, mix in the praline paste, then fold in the corn flakes. Roll out between 2 sheets of greaseproof paper, 36cm x 16cm. Refrigerate until set. Spread the Nutella thinly over the set crispy base and chill.

For The Chocolate Mousse

Bring 250ml of cream to the boil. Whisk the yolks and sugar together, pour the boiled cream over, return to the pan and heat, stirring, to 80°C. Remove from the heat. Add the chocolate and stir until melted. Semi-whip the remaining 450ml of cream. When the chocolate mixture has cooled to 45°C, fold in the semi-whipped cream.

For The Coconut Jelly (Prepare ahead)

Bring half the coconut milk, lime juice, zest and sugar to the boil. Remove from the heat and stir in the gelatine until dissolved. Add the remaining coconut milk, then pour into the prepared tray. Freeze for 8 hours.

For The Coconut Oil Glaze/Spray

Melt the chocolate gently in a microwave on low power. Whilst still warm, add the coconut oil and stir to dissolve. This can be remelted slowly in the microwave if set.

For The Pineapple And Passion Fruit Sorbet (Prepare ahead)

Bring the sugar and water to the boil, remove from the heat, then add the pineapple and passion fruit. Liquidise with a hand blender, strain, then chill. Once cold, churn in an ice cream machine or use a Pacojet following manufacturer's instructions.

Building The Delice

Place the crispy base into the metal frame, set the sponge on top, press down gently. Top with half the mousse, smooth with a palette knife. Place the frozen jelly on top and press down gently. Smooth over the remaining mousse. Freeze for 4 hours, then cut into 12 portions. Glaze with warm coconut oil glaze or, using a spray gun, coat with the mixture. Refrigerate until serving.

To Serve

Serve as pictured.

046
THE BOAT INN

Walsall Road, Lichfield, WS14 0BU

01543 361 692
www.theboatinnlichfield.com Twitter: @theboatinn_ Instagram: @liamjdillon

B orn in Burton-on-Trent, Liam Dillon is chef and owner of award-winning The Boat Inn in Lichfield, Staffordshire. It was his early memories of his Nana's everyday dinners, cooked for the whole family who had been at work all day, which became a long-lasting memory of how food can be the glue that keeps us together.

Like most within the culinary world, Liam's early experiences of food determined a certain path that has placed him in some of the best restaurants in the UK. With previous experience in some of London's and the world's best kitchens, think Marcus Wareing at The Berkeley, Eleven Madison Park, Daniel, Gilt, Noma, and Tom Sellers' Story, Liam returned to his hometown with the goal of raising the bar of Staffordshire's dining scene via the opening of his first solo venture, The Boat Inn, in 2017.

Liam's cooking is heavily inspired by his travels in Australia where produce was king and these experiences reinvigorated his love for cooking fish and seafood. He has applied the simplicity of cooking with premium ingredients to his menu, serving quality-driven set lunch menus, a solid à la carte menu, and a tasting menu experience for guests who want to treat themselves.

With the launch of the new Versus Series 2019, which sees guest chefs go head-to-head against Liam, he cleverly uses the restaurant to bring big names to the city, so that Lichfield locals can experience their food, opening up their palate to different flavours and techniques, challenging diners to think out of the box. Liam is courting the attentions of a Michelin star, slowly raising the dining standards of the area, and standing proud within the culinary crowd.

"It's taken over two years to find the team that want to be here with me. I feel that only now we are really starting". Liam Dillon

DORSET CRAB, LEEK & NASTURTIUM

SERVES 6

 2016 Clos Ventas, Les Pointes Blanc, 2016,
Languedoc-Roussillon (France)

Ingredients

1 large live crab (1½-2kg)
10 baby leeks
200ml rapeseed oil
Maldon sea salt
1 plum vine tomato
ground black pepper
2 Comice pears
lemon juice (spritz of)
1 punnet nasturtium leaves

How To Remove The Crab Flesh

Cracking the crab in certain places on its body helps to release the meat without creating too much damage to the shell, thus less chance of it getting into the finished product.

Use a knife you aren't too keen on. It doesn't have to be razor sharp and it definitely won't be afterwards.

Remove the crab legs, then break off the tips. Cut through either side with the knife, tapping firmly to go straight through the legs, exposing pure white meat. Push out into a bowl over ice.

The claws are next. The first joint down from the claw is the strongest and needs to be hit on the joint firmly to enable it to be disconnected. Once the top of the claw has been removed, the 2 knuckles and the white meat will be exposed. This can be scooped out with a lobster pick or the thin handle of a spoon.

The claws need a little more attention. I always explain the claw as if it was a human hand. Pull back the 'thumb' carefully and you should be able to remove the shell and the cartilage. If not, it can be removed when the meat is flaked down. Use the knife to strike the main body of the claw. Do this all the way around a couple of times, creating a smooth fracture which will then be easy to move away from the meat. The claws of the crab have the most amount of meat in them, so this is an important stage.

Once all the meat is flaked away from the bone, place it on a flat tray over ice and pick through it to make sure there are no bits of shell.

Method

For The Crab

Steam the crab, then carefully remove the flesh.

Chef's Tip

When preparing the crab, use someone else's knife or an inexpensive one.

For The Charred Leeks

Split the baby leeks down the middle and remove the root. This will give long thin strips of leek. Wash them well to make sure all dirt is removed. Season with rapeseed oil and salt, then blow torch the leeks to char them well.

For The Tomato

There are 2 ways to skin a tomato, the first being dropping it into boiling, salted water for 30 seconds, then into iced water. This will not cook the tomato but will lift the skin from the flesh and allow it to be easily removed. Another way, and the best way for this dish, is to use a blow torch to burn the skin, then wipe the skin off. This gives a better flavour to the tomato. Once the skin is removed, cut the tomato into quarters, then cut out the seeds. Reserve the seeds and all trimmings which can be used with the crab shells for a soup, bisque or sauce. Use a small ring cutter to punch out discs of the tomato flesh. Immediately prior to serving, dress the tomato discs in rapeseed oil and season with salt and pepper.

For The Pear

We use Comice pears because they are beautiful and plump. Dice the pears into 1cm cubes immediately before serving so they don't go brown.

Bringing The Dish Together

Allow about 40-45g of white crab meat per person and place into a mixing bowl. Add a teaspoon of the diced pear to each portion of the crab and season with flaked sea salt, rapeseed oil and lemon juice. Use a ring cutter to neatly place the crab in the centre of a plate. Arrange the charred leeks on the crab and top with the tomato discs. Finish with nasturtium leaves.

COTSWOLD VENISON, CAULIFLOWER & MUSHROOM

SERVES 6

 Blanc Vi Natural Negre Organic, 2016, Vins Petxina, Catalunya (Spain)

Ingredients

Mushroom And Onion Pickle

50ml Champagne vinegar or white wine vinegar
100ml chicken stock or water
50ml rapeseed oil, 25ml lemon juice
saffron (pinch of)
1 sprig thyme, 1 sprig rosemary
2 bay leaves, 2 cloves garlic
6 white peppercorns
coriander seed (pinch of)
Maldon sea salt (pinch of)
100g chestnut mushrooms (sliced)
20 baby pickling onions (peeled)

Venison Marinade

15g juniper (crushed)
25g orange zest, 2g rosemary
400g onions (sliced), 15g garlic
10 black peppercorns
3 bay leaves, 1 bottle red wine

Venison

1kg venison loin, 50g butter, 4 sprigs thyme

Cauliflower Salt

50g juniper, 50g fennel seed
10g star anise, 5g black pepper
150g table salt

Cauliflower Purée And Fried Cauliflower

2 large cauliflower heads
50g butter, 100g fresh yeast
50ml double cream, Maldon sea salt

Potato Terrine

3-5 Maris Piper potatoes (peeled)
200g *clarified butter* (melted)
salt, pepper

Garnish (optional)

pickled elderberries, venison sausages

terrine mould (lined with parchment paper)

Method

For The Mushroom And Onion Pickle (Prepare ahead)
Combine the liquid ingredients. Place the dry ingredients in a large bowl, pour over the liquid and combine well. Add the mushrooms and onions and leave for a minimum of 6 hours.

For The Venison
Place the marinade ingredients, except the wine, into a metal container. Bring the red wine to the boil, then pour over the marinade ingredients and leave to infuse until cold. Place the loin into the marinade for 1 hour, then pat dry and reserve. The marinade can be used a further twice so reserve it for another occasion.

For The Cauliflower Salt
Preheat the oven to 160°C (fan).
Place all the ingredients, except the salt, on a metal tray and oven roast for 8 minutes. Leave to cool slightly, then blitz in a blender and add to the salt.

For The Fried Cauliflower
Remove the larger florets from the cauliflower heads and reserve the trim for the purée. Sprinkle cauliflower salt over the larger florets, leave them to cure for 30 minutes. Rinse well and set aside.

For The Cauliflower Purée
Finely chop the cauliflower trim and *sauté* in butter until it is coloured. Crumble over the yeast and cook for 3 minutes. Stir in the cream and bring to the boil. Remove from the heat and blend to a silky purée. Pass through a fine sieve and season.

For The Potato Terrine
Preheat the oven to 170°C (fan).
Slice the potatoes to 3mm thickness and dress in melted butter. Layer the slices in the terrine mould. After each layer, season with salt and pepper. Once filled, cover with parchment paper and a lid. Bake for 1 hour 40 minutes, or until a knife will go through the terrine with no resistance. Chill the terrine with a weight pressing, if possible. This helps the terrine stay together when reheating.

To Serve
Preheat the oven to 180°C (fan).
Season the venison loin with table salt, then seal all over in a hot pan. Add the butter and fresh thyme. Sit the loin on the thyme sprigs and place in the oven for 8-10 minutes, or when probed to 44°C. Rest for no less than 8 minutes.
Reheat the purée. Deep fry the florets until golden brown. Portion the terrine and reheat in a pan in a little oil.
Serve as pictured. We finish the dish with pickled elderberries.

CHOCOLATE PARFAIT, MILK & MALT

SERVES 6

 Chapoutier Bila-Haut Banyuls 2016 Rimage (France)

Ingredients

Chocolate Parfait

220g pasteurised egg yolk
330ml water
45g liquid glucose
680ml double cream
135g milk powder
650g Caramélia milk chocolate

White Chocolate Aero

500g white chocolate
10g mycro (cocoa butter)
2g glycerin syrup
20g vegetable oil

Malt Ice Cream

200g egg yolks
200g sugar
500ml whole milk
500ml double cream
20g liquid glucose
200g malt extract

Salted Caramel

70g glucose
725g sugar
600ml double cream
18g Maldon sea salt
60g butter

Crystallised Rice

135g caster sugar
270ml water
100g puffed rice

Wet Milk Skin

500ml whole milk
50g milk powder

Spraying Chocolate (Optional)

60g dark chocolate
40g cocoa butter

1 litre syphon gun and 2 N2O chargers

Method

For The Chocolate Parfait (Prepare ahead)

Whip the yolks until fluffy in a Kitchen Aid. Boil the water and glucose, then pour over the yolks slowly while whisking.
Bring 120ml of cream and the milk powder to the boil, pour over the chocolate and mix until melted. Stir into the whipped yolks.
Whip the remaining cream to soft peaks, then stir into the chocolate until smooth. Freeze in your desired moulds.

For The White Chocolate Aero (Prepare ahead)

Melt 300g of the chocolate to 40°C in a *bain-marie*, add the other ingredients, except the chocolate. Once fully incorporated, add the remaining chocolate and allow to cool to 28-31°C.

Warm the syphon gun slightly, then pour the mixture into it. Charge the gun with both gas canisters, then spray into a small vacuum container with a lid. Remove the air from the chamber with a pump or place into a vac pack machine to remove the air. Once the air has been removed, the mixture should have expanded to fill the vacuum container. Freeze overnight, cut into portions and store in the freezer.

For The Malt Ice Cream

Whisk the yolks and sugar together. Bring the milk, cream and glucose to the boil, then pour over the yolk mixture. Combine well, then return to the heat and bring to 82°C. Add the malt extract, then churn in an ice cream machine, or transfer into a Pacojet container and freeze.

For The Salted Caramel

Bring the glucose and sugar to a caramel. Carefully pour in the cream while whisking the mixture off the heat. Bring to the boil to dissolve the sugar. Pass through a fine sieve, then stir in the salt and butter. Allow to cool.

For The Crystallised Rice

Bring the sugar and water to 118°C. Stir in the rice over a low heat, stirring until the sugar crystallises.

For The Wet Milk Skin

Gently heat the ingredients over a low heat to 84°C until a skin forms, about 15-20 minutes. Remove the skin and reserve in milk in the fridge.

For The Spraying Chocolate (Optional)

Melt the spraying chocolate ingredients, add to a warm spraying gun and spray the parfait until totally covered.

To Assemble

Allow the parfait to warm a little so it is not too hard when served. Serve as pictured.

056
CARTERS OF MOSELEY

2C Wake Green Road, Moseley, Birmingham, B13 9EZ

0121 449 8885
www.cartersofmoseley.co.uk
Twitter: @cartersmoseley Facebook: Carters of Moseley Instagram: cartersofmoseley

He could have been an MC. Or, rather, for a while he was. Brad Carter used to get ravers to throw up their hands in the air (like they just didn't care) before settling on a career in the kitchen.

The Brummie raver-turned-Michelin-starred-chef found his calling after cooking in kitchens across the Second City. He met his long-term partner, Holly, when their paths crossed at a local restaurant and together, they launched Carters of Moseley.

Initially, Brad worked long hours, frequently sleeping on the floor, but he made the breakthrough when he won a Good Food Guide Award for Readers' Restaurant of the Year. He received the gong from Nathan Outlaw and suddenly things started to move.

Michelin started to take an interest and not long after, Brad took a call from the Guide's editor. He was cutting an ox heart when she told him he was about to receive a star - and at first he didn't believe it.

Since then he has further finessed his uniquely British food while also picking up an Olive Award for being Britain's Most Sustainable Restaurant.

"We're proud of what we've done and of how far we've come. But if Carters of Moseley is about anything, it's about evolution," says Brad. "We're continuing to push by searching out unique, British ingredients so that we don't have to import from all around the world. We're doing something different: creating beautiful British food that's totally modern and also respects the planet."

It has been a recipe for success - for critics and diners alike.

The philosophy of Carters of Moseley is to be a true expression of British terroir within the moment; led by the season and inspired by the producers who work the British landscape.

CHICKEN LIVER, CEREAL

MAKES 60 AMUSE-BOUCHE SIZE PORTIONS

 3 Fonteinen, Oude Geuze, Cuvée Armand & Gaston 2017 (Belgium)

Ingredients

Chicken Liver

3 large banana shallots (sliced)
400ml Madeira
200ml port
2 bay leaves
2 sprigs thyme
1 clove garlic (crushed)
500g chicken livers (before trimming)
15g pink salt
4 large eggs
350g butter (melted, cooled)

Cereal

60g goose fat
180g jumbo oats (sieved)
300g sunflower seeds
200g linseed
50g cocoa nibs
thyme leaves (to taste)
14g salt
50g sugar
100g seedless golden raisins

enamel terrine dish
large gastronorm tray

Method

For The Chicken Liver

Place the shallots, Madeira, port, herbs and garlic in a pan. Simmer slowly to cook the shallots and reduce the liquids, about 1½ hours. Remove the thyme and bay leaves, leave to cool.

Remove all the sinew from the liver (about 100g weight loss). Put the liver and shallot reduction in a Thermomix or strong blender and blend for 3 minutes at speed 7-8. Add the salt and eggs and blend for 1 minute more. Pour the butter in through the lid and keep blending until all the mixture is smooth and *emulsified*.

Preheat the oven to 85°C (combi).

Brush a sheet of cling film with oil and line the terrine dish, with the oil against the enamel sides. Pass the liver base into the terrine through a fine sieve. Pull up the sides of the film to prevent air pockets forming. Fit the lid on the terrine and cook for 75 minutes. The parfait will be cooked but still soft and pipeable (for a slicing style of pâté, cook it for 15 minutes longer). Cool, then fill a piping bag with the mixture. Chill until needed, serve at room temperature.

For The Cereal

Preheat the oven to 180°C.

Melt the goose fat on a large gastronorm tray. Combine all the other ingredients, except for the raisins. Toss the mixture in the hot fat - it should cover the tray in a thin layer. Bake for 21 minutes. Add the raisins and put it back in the oven to bake for 3 minutes more. Cool, store in a sealed container.

To Serve

Pipe about 15g of the chicken liver parfait over the base of a small bowl and sprinkle a thin layer of the cereal on top. Serve with a teaspoon.

SMOKED TAMWORTH PORK, CABBAGE, SHISHITO PEPPERS

SERVES 4

 Christian Tschida, Hokus Pokus, Burgenland, 2017 (Austria)

Ingredients

Smoked Tamworth Pork

1 tbsp salt

1 tbsp light brown sugar

500g Tamworth pork neck, or best you can find

Cabbage And Shishito Peppers

500ml water

375g unsalted butter (diced)

1 tbsp apple cider vinegar

6g salt

1g xanthan gum

1 Hispi or sweetheart cabbage (outer leaves removed, heart thinly sliced)

4 shishito peppers (finely sliced)

smoker

BBQ

Method

For The Smoked Tamworth Pork

Set up a smoker to 110°C.

Combine the salt and sugar, then rub it into the pork until evenly coated.

Add the pork to the smoker and cook for around 1½ hours until the pork reaches 65°C on a temperature probe.

Rest in a warm place for around 30 minutes.

For The Cabbage And Shishito Peppers

While the pork is resting, boil the water, then add the butter, vinegar, salt and xanthan gum and blitz in a blender on high for 2 minutes until smooth. Pass the butter *emulsion* through a fine sieve into a clean saucepan and cover with a lid.

Bring the butter *emulsion* to the boil, add the cabbage and peppers, cover with a lid and reduce the heat slightly. Cook the cabbage until softened and the peppers just enough so they still have bite, around 2 minutes.

To Finish And Serve

Set up the BBQ to direct heat, with hot coals. Grill the pork all over until charred evenly, place on a chopping board and carve into 4 thick slices.

Place a slice of the pork on each plate, then cover with the cabbage, peppers and a little of the butter sauce.

BLACK RICE & KELP ICE CREAM

SERVES 4

Fukuju, Awasaki Sparkling Sake, Nada
(Japan)

Method

For The Black Rice And Kelp Ice Cream (Prepare 1 day ahead)

Preheat the oven to 180°C.

Roast the rice and kelp for 12 minutes, then blend the rice to a coarse powder. Set aside in a container with the whole piece of kelp.

Heat the milk and cream to 84°C. Using a hand blender, mix in all the ingredients except the rice and kelp. Pour the warm mixture over the kelp and rice and leave to infuse overnight.

The next day, pass through a *chinois*, then blend again with a hand blender to *emulsify*. Churn in an ice cream machine until set and store in the freezer.

For The Garnish

Heat the oil up to 200-210°C in a saucepan on the stove.

Add the black rice and cook for 20 seconds or until it puffs up and floats on the top of the oil. Drain immediately and discard the oil, set aside to cool.

Preheat the oven to 180°C.

Roast the kelp for 10 minutes. Separate into 2 halves, then crush one half with a rolling pin until you have flakes, set aside to cool.

Place the remaining half in a blender and blitz on full power for 8-10 minutes to a powder. Set aside.

To Serve

Scoop some ice cream into a bowl and squash it to the side of a frozen bowl. Sprinkle with the puffed black rice and the kelp flakes to cover. Finish with a dusting of the powdered seaweed and serve immediately.

Chef's Tip

This is best served in frozen bowls so pop your bowls in the freezer a few hours before serving.

Ingredients

Black Rice And Kelp Ice Cream

60g black rice
1 piece kelp
600ml whole milk
125ml whipping cream
20g milk powder
12g trimoline
1g ice cream stabiliser
1g xanthan gum
90g caster sugar
35g liquid glucose

Garnish

250ml grapeseed oil
50g black rice
50g kelp

066
CHEAL'S OF HENLEY

64 High Street, Henley-in-Arden, Warwickshire, B95 5BX

01564 793 856
www.chealsofhenley.co.uk Twitter: @Chealshenley
Instagram: chealsofhenley Facebook: Cheal's of Henley

Located on the famous 'Henley Mile' High Street in 'Shakespeare's County', Cheal's sits amongst many historic buildings, some of which date back to medieval times, in one of England's oldest market towns.

Owner Matt Cheal has always been interested in food, having grown up in his family's hotel, where he started work at the tender age of 13. Matt's talent and passion for cooking became apparent and developed, even though his parents Tony and Julie tried to dissuade him against a career which is renowned for long, antisocial hours! After college, Matt trained and worked in Michelin-starred Simpsons restaurant in Birmingham, starting as a commis chef and working his way up to head chef.

In 2002, Matt won the British Culinary Federation Junior Chef of the Year, following that up in 2010 by winning the Federation's Senior Chef of the Year. To date, Matt is the only chef to have won both accolades.

Together with his wife Emma and parents Tony and Julie, Matt wanted to open and run a fine dining restaurant in Warwickshire. When the property in Henley became available, they realised it was the perfect venue to create Cheal's of Henley.

Following a complete refurbishment of the beautiful, old, beamed building, Cheal's opened in October 2015. It is now an elegant dining space with 30 covers in the main restaurant and 12 covers in the separate private dining area.

When Matt talks about his restaurant you quickly hear his passion for the team's food; he is very proud of what they all achieve and explains that this can only be continued by each individual playing their part working together as a single team. The hard work and dedication of his team, together with support from his family, speaks volumes in the many positive reviews received from satisfied diners.

Cheal's food is seasonally sourced from Warwickshire suppliers who specialise in rare breeds of meats and game. They use local ingredients, some of which are grown on the nearby Cheal's allotment, tended by kitchen member Caroline Stockley, who supplies fresh ingredients daily.

WHIPPED CHICKEN LIVER, STRAWBERRY SALSA VERDE, RED ONION, CHICORY, THYME HOBNOB

SERVES 4

🍷 *Clos Saint Landelin, Gewurztraminer,*
2010 (France)

Ingredients

Chicken Liver Parfait
100ml ruby port
500g liver
25g pink salt, 10g Maldon salt
1 onion (diced)
double cream (dash of)
60g egg yolks
100g egg white
8 leaves gelatine (softened in cold water)
600g butter (melted)

Thyme Hobnobs
1 onion (diced)
150g butter
1 tbsp golden syrup
150g self-raising flour
100g caster sugar
120g oats
1 tbsp bicarbonate of soda
20g fresh thyme (chopped)
salt (pinch of)

Strawberry Salsa Verde
1 tbsp diced strawberries
1 tbsp tomatoes (*concasse*)
1 tbsp diced shallot
1 tbsp chopped chervil
1 tbsp vinaigrette
season (to taste)

Pickled Red Onion
100ml white wine vinegar
100g sugar
100ml water
1 red onion (thinly sliced)

To Serve
chicory leaves

Method

For The Chicken Liver Parfait

Reduce the port by half.

Combine the liver with the salts, mix well and vac pack. Place in a water bath for 10 minutes.

Sweat the onion until soft, add a dash of cream, then stir in the reduced port.

Add the yolks and whites to a blender. Add the cooked livers, bloomed gelatine and the onion/port mixture. Blend until smooth, with the melted butter, until *emulsified* and it reaches 62°C. Pass through a fine sieve, transfer to a piping bag and chill.

For The Thyme Hobnobs

Sweat the onion until soft. Melt the butter and syrup in a pan.

Add the dried ingredients and thyme to a mixer bowl. Place on half speed and combine with the butter mixture. Season with salt. Roll into ballotines and chill.

Preheat the oven to 160°C (fan).

Slice the ballotine into discs and bake for 8 minutes.

> **Chef's Tip**
>
> If you make the biscuits in advance, gently warm them through before eating for added indulgence.

For The Strawberry Salsa Verde

Dress the ingredients with the vinaigrette, season to taste.

For The Pickled Red Onion

Bring the vinegar, sugar and water to the boil, then leave to cool. Place the onion into the pickling *liquor* and leave for 3 hours.

To Serve

Pipe a small amount of parfait on the centre of the plate. Arrange the pickled red onion, strawberry salsa verde and chicory leaves over the top, trying to get as much height as possible. Warm the hobnobs in the oven for 30 seconds.

CANNON & SHOULDER OF LAMB, GOAT'S CURD, AUBERGINE & MISO, CARROT

SERVES 4

 Château Palmer, Alter Ego De Palmer, 2014 (France)

Ingredients

4 x 120g cannons of lamb (fat on)

Lamb Shoulder

1 shoulder of lamb (boned, rolled)
200g basic *mirepoix* (carrots, celery, onion, garlic, thyme, rosemary)
150ml Madeira wine
200ml white wine
800ml chicken stock
200ml veal stock

Aubergine And Miso Purée

1 shallot (diced)
1 clove garlic (diced)
1 aubergine (diced)
olive oil (glug of)
40ml rice vinegar
40g Demerara sugar
100g miso
50g butter

Carrots

500g duck fat
4 carrots (peeled)
2 sprigs thyme
2 cloves garlic

Goat's Curd

200g goat's curd
20g plain flour
1 egg (whisked)
50g panko breadcrumbs
salt and pepper
oil (to deep fry)

Garnish

fresh micro coriander leaves

Method

For The Lamb Cannons

Remove any excess fat and score with a sharp boning knife.

Melt the excess fat in a hot pan, then chill.

Place the cannons in small, individual vac pack bags with a small amount of chilled, rendered lamb fat. Cook at 58°C for 45 minutes, then chill in an ice bath.

> **Chef's Tip**
>
> Any fat or liquid in the vac pack bags left from cooking the lamb can be whisked into the sauce prior to serving for extra flavour.

For The Lamb Shoulder (For best results, cook the day before)

Preheat the oven to 90°C (fan).

Seal the lamb in a hot pan until golden brown all over. Remove, add the *mirepoix* and sweat without colour. After 5 minutes of regular stirring, add the alcohols and reduce by half. Return the lamb to the pan, pour in the stocks, cover and cook in the oven for 7 hours. Leave to cool for 30 minutes, then refrigerate until the liquid sets.

For The Aubergine And Miso Purée

Sweat the shallot and garlic until soft with no colour. Remove from the pan, add the aubergine and sweat in the oil, without colouring, until soft. Add the vinegar, sugar and miso and cook for 20 minutes. Blend with the butter, then pass through a fine sieve.

For The Carrots

Put the duck fat in a pan and *temper* to 130°C. Place the carrots in the pan with the thyme and garlic and cook until soft. Cut the carrots down the middle from top to bottom and seal in a pan to add colour.

For The Goat's Curd

Season the goat's curd and roll into 8g balls. *Pané* the balls by rolling in flour, then egg and finally breadcrumbs. Deep fry at 190°C for 30 seconds.

To Serve

Place the lamb cannons in a hot pan, fat-side down. *Render* the fat, adding a nice colour. Transfer to the oven (225°C fan) for 4 minutes. Remove the lamb shoulder from the stock, cut a thin slice and seal in a hot non-stick pan until golden brown. Serve as pictured.

LICHFIELD STRAWBERRIES, WHITE CHOCOLATE MOUSSE, SABLE BISCUIT, STRAWBERRY SORBET

SERVES 4

 Elysium Black Muscat, 2015, California (USA)

Ingredients

Strawberry Sorbet

500g ripe strawberries
10ml lemon juice
200g caster sugar
200ml water
1½ tbsp liquid glucose

White Chocolate Mousse

100g white chocolate
100g tofu

Sablé Biscuit

500g butter
300g sugar
40g egg yolk
1 lemon (zest of)
600g pastry flour

To Serve

fresh strawberries (chopped)
apple marigold

Method

For The Strawberry Sorbet

Blend the strawberries and lemon juice to a purée. Place in a pan and reduce by half. Pass through a fine sieve and leave to cool.

Place the sugar, water and glucose into a pan, bring to a simmer and maintain for 5 minutes. Leave to cool.

Combine both mixtures, then churn in an ice cream machine for 45 minutes.

For The White Chocolate Mousse

Melt the chocolate. Blend the tofu, then slowly *emulsify* the chocolate into the tofu. Transfer to a piping back and leave to set in the fridge.

For The Sablé Biscuit

Preheat the oven to 160°C (fan).

Cream the butter, sugar, egg yolk and lemon zest. Mix the flour in, then roll between 2 sheets of parchment paper. Chill in the fridge.

Bake for 8 minutes or until golden. Use a cutter to cut out discs whilst still hot.

To Serve

Place the sablé biscuit on the base, pipe the white chocolate mousse in a crown around the biscuit.

Add some chopped fresh strawberries and a *quenelle* of strawberry sorbet. Garnish with apple marigold.

Chef's Tip

Use a warm spoon to *quenelle* your sorbet for a perfectly smooth finish.

076
THE CHERRY HOUSE AT WERRINGTON

125 Church Street, Werrington, Peterborough, PE4 6QF

01733 571 721
www.cherryhouserestaurant.co.uk Twitter: @cherryhouse125

Less than five miles from the centre of the cathedral city of Peterborough is the delightful Cherry House at Werrington restaurant. Close enough to be accessible for the growing population of the city and its surrounding towns and villages, yet far enough away to provide calm and tranquility in a 400-year-old, Grade II listed, English cottage with historic links to Oliver Cromwell and to Cherry Farm, famous for its Werrington cherries.

Under the ownership of chef patron Andrew Corrick, formerly head chef at The Park Lane Hotel in Mayfair, The Cherry House offers classic dining, taking influences from French and British cuisine and making the most of some of the exceptional ingredients produced in the East of England. Andrew took over the restaurant, with its three separate dining areas and lounge, 25 years ago and has a long-serving team front of house, now ably managed by son Jordan and a small number of chefs working alongside him.

The Cherry House at Werrington offers something for serious food lovers, for romantic evenings, celebrations and gatherings, and for families simply enjoying fine fresh food prepared with care and attention to detail. The team places great emphasis on respectful but friendly hospitality and enjoys a reputation that has spread far and wide.

For 25 years, Andrew and his team have been producing classic dishes with British and French influences.

MOSAIC OF ENGLISH ASPARAGUS, SWEET PEPPERS & SUN KISSED TOMATOES, TOMATO SALSA

SERVES 4

Paul Cluver Gewürztraminer (South Africa)

Ingredients

Jelly

250ml Alsace wine
5 leaves gelatine (soaked in cold water)

Mosaic

1 large red pepper
1 large yellow pepper
1 large orange pepper
10 asparagus spears
250g sun-kissed tomatoes (drained)
seasoning

Tomato Salsa

4 vine plum tomatoes
1 tbsp brown sugar
1 banana shallot (finely chopped)
1 clove garlic (crushed)
250ml dry white wine
2 tbsp white wine vinegar
150ml extra virgin olive oil
seasoning
1 tsp chives (finely snipped)

To Serve

24 asparagus tips
chives
terrine mould (lined with cling film, chilled)

Method

For The Jelly

Bring the wine to the boil, remove from the heat, then add the soaked gelatine. Pass through a fine sieve and set aside to cool.

For The Mosaic

Blanch, skin and deseed the peppers. Lightly boil the asparagus, remove from the water and cool.

When the jelly has cooled, pour a small layer in the mould to cover the bottom and set in the fridge. Set a layer of asparagus, topped with sun-kissed tomatoes, then top with jelly and season. Refrigerate until set. When set, arrange a layer of yellow peppers, top with jelly and set in the fridge. Repeat the steps with the red pepper and orange pepper. Refrigerate until set.

Chef's Tip

Allow the jelly in the mosaic to set fully before you attempt to slice it.

For The Tomato Salsa

Blanch, peel and deseed the vine tomatoes. Cut into *concasse*.

Place the sugar into a small pan with a little water and caramelise.

When caramelised, add the shallot, garlic, wine and vinegar and reduce by two-thirds, then add the tomato *concasse*, olive oil and season to taste. Allow to cool, then stir in the chives.

To Serve

Slice the mosaic with a sharp carving knife, then lay on a plate. Dress with the tomato salsa, serve with asparagus tips and garnish with chives.

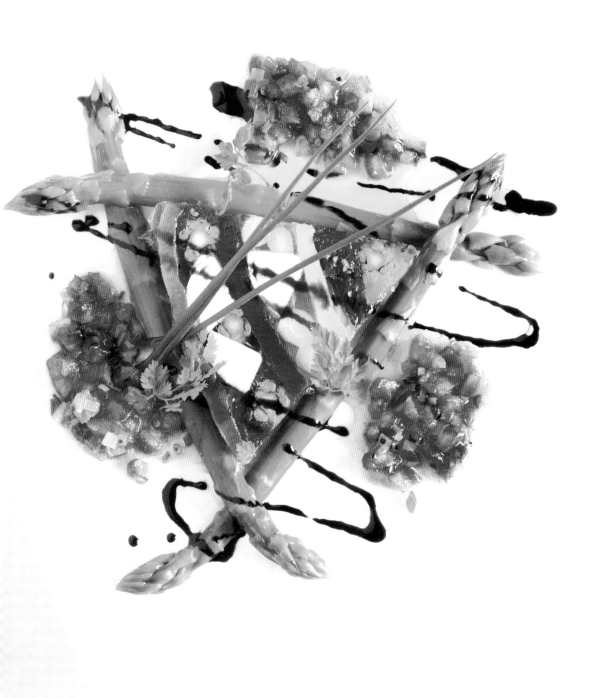

CANNON OF ENGLISH LAMB, SWEET POTATO & STILTON GRATIN

SERVES 4

 Château Les Eyquem Margaux (France)

Ingredients

Lamb

4 cannons of lamb (best end eyes)
olive oil (drizzle of)
2 sprigs rosemary (chopped)
seasoning

Sweet Potato And Stilton Gratin

500g sweet potato (peeled)
300ml double cream
1 clove garlic (crushed)
200g Stilton (grated)
seasoning

Lamb Sauce

1 banana shallot (finely chopped)
1 clove garlic (crushed)
4 sprigs rosemary (finely chopped)
300ml good quality red wine
500ml lamb stock
1 litre veal jus
2 tsp redcurrant jelly
50g unsalted butter (cold, cubed)

Vegetables

12 pieces *turned* carrots (cooked *al dente*)
12 pieces *turned* courgettes (cooked *al dente*)
12 pieces *turned* butternut squash (cooked *al dente*)
12 asparagus tips (cooked *al dente*)
8 stalks Tender-stem broccoli (cooked *al dente*)
butter (knob of)

Garnish

4 sprigs rosemary
4 sprigs parsley

Method

To Prepare The Lamb

Trim the cannon of fat and sinews, leaving just the eye of meat.

For The Sweet Potato And Stilton Gratin

Preheat the oven to 200°C.

Slice the sweet potatoes on a mandoline, 2-3cm thick.

Gently heat the cream in a small pan then whisk in the garlic.

Butter a suitable sized oven dish and season. Place a layer of sweet potatoes in the dish making sure to overlap. Cover with the cream and garlic mixture. Sprinkle with the grated Stilton and season. Repeat layering twice more. Bake in the oven for 20-25 minutes until the potatoes are soft.

For The Lamb Sauce

Sweat off the shallot, garlic and rosemary, allow to colour slightly.

Add the red wine and reduce to a glaze. Pour in the lamb stock and reduce fully. Add the veal jus and reduce by two-thirds. Stir in the redcurrant jelly and simmer until it has melted into the sauce. Set aside.

To Cook The Lamb

Preheat the oven to 200°C.

Seal the lamb cannons in a pan on the stove top with a little olive oil and chopped rosemary, season well.

Place in the oven for 6-8 minutes, then remove from the oven and allow to rest.

Chef's Tip

Cook the lamb pink and allow it to rest.

To Finish And To Serve

Slice the rested cannons and arrange on plates. Cut the potato gratin into rounds. Reheat the *blanched* vegetables, butter and season well, then arrange on the plates. Bring the sauce to the boil, check the seasoning and whisk in the butter. Pass through a fine sieve, then pour over the lamb. Garnish with a sprig of rosemary and parsley.

MELANGE A TROIS

SERVES 4

 The Noble Wrinkled Riesling, McLaren Vale (Australia)

Ingredients

Summer Puddings

400g mixed frozen berries
50g caster sugar
10 medium slices bread (preferably a couple of days old, crusts removed)

Chocolate Ganache

375ml double cream
440g dark chocolate callets (55% cocoa solids)
3 egg yolks
50g icing sugar

Brandy Snaps

55ml golden syrup
55g Demerara sugar
55g butter
50g plain flour (sieved)
½ tsp ground ginger (sieved)
¼ lemon (juice of)

Raspberry Mille-Feuille Filling

2 punnets raspberries
500ml double cream (whipped)

To Serve

chocolate sauce
clotted cream (small tub of)
8 raspberries
8 blueberries
4 sprigs redcurrants
4 strawberries
4 blackberries
4 sprigs mint
icing sugar (for dusting)

4 small pudding basins
4 pastry rings or small moulds
12 stainless steel ring moulds (greased)

Method

For The Summer Puddings (Prepare ahead)

Place the frozen berries and sugar in a pan with a little water, bring to the boil, then set aside to cool.

Cut the bread into strips to fit the pudding basins.

Transfer the cool berries to a fine sieve and leave to drain. Dip the bread strips into the syrup and line the moulds. Fill the moulds with the berries and top with more dipped bread. Refrigerate overnight.

Liquidise the remaining berries and syrup. Pass through a fine sieve to make the coulis that will cover the puddings.

For The Chocolate Ganache

Place 200ml of the cream in a small pan and bring almost to the boil. Turn down the heat and fold in the chocolate. Remove from the heat when smooth.

Place the yolks and sugar in a bowl and whisk with an electric whisk until pale. Pour over the chocolate and cream mixture and continue to whisk until fully incorporated. Set aside to cool.

Whip the remaining cream to soft peaks, then fold into the chocolate mixture. Transfer to pastry rings or small moulds and set in the fridge.

For The Brandy Snaps

Preheat the oven to 220°C.

Place the syrup, sugar and butter in a small pan and sit over a low heat. Stir until smooth.

Stir the flour and ginger into the mix, add the lemon juice and mix until smooth. Set aside and allow to cool.

Place the ring moulds on a baking tray lined with a silicone mat. Roll a teaspoon of the mix into a ball, then flatten into each ring. Bake until golden brown, about 6-8 minutes. Remove from the oven, then remove the steel rings to give 12 perfect brandy snap discs. Set aside to cool.

To Serve

Remove the ganache and summer puddings from the moulds.

Place on a plate with some chocolate sauce around the ganache. Pour the berry coulis over the summer puddings. Layer the brandy snap discs with whipped cream and fresh raspberries. Serve as pictured with a *quenelle* of clotted cream. Decorate with the berries, sprigs of mint and finish with a dusting of icing sugar.

Chef's Tip

The finest ingredients from the chocolate to the berries will make this dish.

086
CRAFT DINING ROOMS

Unit 10 The ICC, 8 Centenary Square, Birmingham, B1 2EA

0121 655 5550
www.craftdiningrooms.co.uk Twitter: @craftdiningrooms Facebook: Craft Dining Rooms

I n Craft Dining Rooms they are passionate about quality British produce.

Craft Dining Rooms is a distinctly unique dining experience. Everything is handcrafted, artisan in nature and skillfully selected. From the food, the drinks, the decor and even their logo. They champion only the best of British and bring you a unique dining experience, every time.

They have carefully selected their partners from the finest British artisans, producers and suppliers. All the produce is chosen for its superior quality and sustainable nature. The menu will be ever evolving and reflective of the best seasonable produce from British farmers, cheesemongers, brewers, distillers and vintners.

Owners Sam and Emma Morgan head up the team and award-winning chef director Tom Wells leads the kitchen. Tom's previous employers include Tom Aitkens and Luke Mangan.

The Craft Dining Rooms menu features the team's modern take on a few well-loved dishes alongside some brand-new creations that make the most of local ingredients.

From born to bred, field to fork and grape to glass. This is the Craft Dining Experience.

CRAFTED TOGETHER
WITH THE GREAT
ARTISANS OF BRITAIN.

FROM BORN TO BRED,
FIELD TO FORK AND
GRAPE TO GLASS.

—

THIS IS THE
CRAFT DINING
EXPERIENCE.

High-end British artisan cuisine showcasing the finest producers in Britain.

LOBSTER SOUP, CRISPY CLAW, SEA VEGETABLES

SERVES 4

 Shoreline 2017, Lyme Bay, Devon (England)

Ingredients

Lobster
1 carrot, ½ leek
1 onion, 3 cloves garlic
20g lemon thyme
200ml white wine
30ml white wine vinegar
8 black peppercorns
water, 2 lobsters

Crispy Lobster Claw
cooked lobster claw
100g plain flour, 3 eggs (beaten)
150g panko breadcrumbs
oil (for deep frying)

Lobster Soup
400g lobster shells
1 carrot (peeled, diced)
1 onion (peeled, diced)
1 leek (washed, diced), 3 cloves garlic
sunflower oil (drizzle of)
800ml shellfish stock
200ml double cream, 20g tarragon
100g unsalted butter (cold, diced)

Lobster Oil
300g lobster shells
500ml sunflower oil
3 star anise, 10 black peppercorns
5g coriander seeds
1 vanilla pod (split), 1 orange (zest of)

Lobster Emulsion
6 eggs, 500ml lobster oil
shellfish stock (if needed)

Sea Vegetables
10g samphire, 10g sea aster
10g sea rosemary, 10g oyster leaf
butter (knob of)

Method

For The Lobster
Place all the ingredients, except the lobsters, in a large pan and bring to the boil. When boiling, *blanch* the lobsters for 2 minutes each, then allow to cool naturally. Remove the meat from the shells. Keep the shells for stock and lobster oil.

Chef's Tip
Make sure your lobsters are alive and alert when you buy them; remember the fresher the better!

For The Crispy Lobster Claw
Pané the claws in flour, egg, then the panko.

For The Lobster Soup
Preheat the oven to 180°C (fan).

Roast the lobster shells for 10 minutes.

Sauté the vegetables and garlic in oil until tender, add the lobster shells and cook for 5 minutes. Pour in the stock and bring to the boil. Reduce by a quarter, then add the double cream and tarragon. Simmer again, then blend in a powerful blender and pass through a fine *chinois*. Adjust the seasoning, pass again, then rapidly chill.

When ready to serve, bring to the boil and finish with cold butter. Blend with a stick blender to give a foamy soup.

For The Lobster Oil
Add all the ingredients to a large pan. Gently warm the oil, then leave to infuse somewhere warm for 4 hours. Blend the oil with a stick blender, then pass through a muslin cloth and store until needed.

For The Lobster Emulsion
Boil the eggs for 6 minutes, then refresh in iced water. Place in a blender and gradually blend in the lobster oil until it looks like mayonnaise. Add a little shellfish stock to loosen if needed, pass through a sieve and store until needed.

To Serve
Gently roast the lobster tail in butter until hot. Deep fry (180°C) the claw until golden and crispy. *Sauté* the sea vegetables gently in butter.

Place half a lobster tail in the middle of a bowl with a large dot of lobster *emulsion* and arrange the sea vegetables as pictured. Serve the lobster soup and crispy claw on the side.

BEEF WELLINGTON

SERVES 4

 *La Colonia, Malbec*
(Argentina)

Ingredients

Beef
500g fillet of beef
oil (drizzle of), salt and pepper

Mushroom Duxelle
400g chestnut mushrooms (sliced)
oil (small drizzle of)
½ small onion (finely diced)
1 clove garlic (finely chopped)
2 sprigs thyme
1 tsp tarragon (finely chopped)
1 tsp parsley (finely chopped)
1 tsp chives (finely chopped)
salt and freshly ground black pepper

To Build The Wellington
6 slices Parma ham
250g puff pastry (rolled to a 30cm square)
1 egg (beaten)

Salt Pastry
(ingredients combined, then refrigerate for 1 hour)
600g salt, 400g plain flour
160g egg white, 160ml cold water

Caramelised Onion
salt pastry, 4 large onions
150g wild mushrooms
20g chives (finely chopped)

Creamed Potato
6 large Maris Piper potatoes (washed, baked)
150g unsalted butter (softened)
150ml whole milk (warm), salt (pinch of)

Red Wine Sauce
50ml sunflower oil
200g beef trimmings
100g shallots (finely sliced)
150g button mushrooms (finely sliced)
1 bulb garlic (halved), 25g thyme, 10g tarragon
5 black peppercorns, 500ml red wine
300ml port, 1 litre veal stock

blow torch

Method

For The Beef
Preheat a heavy-based frying pan over a high heat. Add a drizzle of oil and sear the fillet on all sides. Lightly season, then wrap tightly in cling film and chill for 10 minutes. Remove the film.

For The Mushroom Duxelle And To Build The Wellington
In the same pan, fry the mushrooms in the oil until dry. Add the onion, garlic and thyme, cook for 1 minute. Turn up the heat, cook until dry. Remove the whole thyme sprigs, stir in the herbs and season. Roughly chop the mixture to achieve a coarse 'duxelle'.

Place the Parma ham, overlapping slightly, onto a sheet of cling film. Cover with the mushrooms, leaving a 1cm gap at the edges.

Place the fillet onto the edge of the duxelle and roll it, making sure it's fully covered with ham all the way around. Leave to set in the fridge for 10 minutes.

Place the pastry on a flour-dusted worktop. Cut a T-shape and place the fillet on the horizontal part. Fold over the ends, then roll the fillet in the vertical part of the 'T'. Brush with beaten egg. Roll a lattice pastry cutter over the pastry trim, then place on the Wellington. Brush again with egg.

Preheat the oven to 225°C (fan).

Set on a tray lined with parchment and bake for 10 minutes, then lower the temperature to 200°C (fan) and cook for 20 minutes for medium. Add another 10 minutes for well done. Leave to rest for 10 minutes before carving.

For The Caramelised Onion
Preheat the oven to 180°C (fan).

Wrap the onions in a salt pastry crust and bake for 45 minutes. Allow to cool, then remove from the crust. Cut off the tops and scoop the onion out whole from the skins, cut into rings. Glaze to a golden colour using a blow torch.

When ready to serve, *sauté* the onion centres until golden and mix with wild mushrooms and chives. Place the onion mix in the base of the onion rings to serve.

For The Creamed Potato
Pass the potato flesh through a drum sieve into a clean pan. Gradually beat in the butter and milk on the heat until the potato is rich and creamy. Season with salt.

For The Red Wine Sauce
Heat the oil in a large pan, *sauté* the beef trimmings until well coloured. Add the shallots and mushrooms and cook until golden. Add the garlic, herbs, peppercorns and wine. Reduce until glossy. Add the port and reduce. Pour in the stock and reduce to a sauce consistency. Pass through a fine *chinois*, adjust the seasoning.

To Serve
Serve as pictured.

BAKEWELL TART SOUFFLE

SERVES 4

Blackthorn Cocktail - Craft Dining Room
35ml sloe gin, 20ml Somerset brandy, 25ml lemon
juice, 10ml gomme syrup (tree sap syrup). Shaken
and served over ice.

Ingredients

Confit Cherries

150g English red cherries (washed)
300ml water
300ml cherry juice
350g caster sugar

Cherry Compôte

150g confit cherries
5g ascorbic acid
Maldon sea salt (to taste)

Frangipane Soufflé Base

500ml whole milk
60g cherry syrup (from confit cherries)
100g caster sugar
10g vanilla extract
100g egg yolk
30g pastry flour
15g cornflour
175g roasted almond butter
Maldon sea salt (to taste)

Soufflé Mix

40g caster sugar
100g egg whites
100g soufflé base
confit cherries
flaked almonds (sprinkling of)
icing sugar (to dust)

Almond Ice Cream

900ml whole milk
300ml double cream
200g caster sugar
70g dextrose
2g Maldon sea salt
100g toasted almonds
120g Sosa Procrema

4 soufflé moulds (buttered)

Method

For The Confit Cherries

Remove the cherry stones and slice into halves. Bring the water and cherry juice to the boil and add the cherries. Keep the heat on the lowest setting and add a teaspoon of sugar every 15 minutes. Cook until cherries are soft and *liquor* has reduced to a syrup.

For The Cherry Compôte

Drain off the confit cherries and blend with the ascorbic acid until a chunky jam texture has been obtained. Season accordingly with the salt.

For The Frangipane Soufflé Base

Place the milk, cherry syrup, 50g of the sugar and vanilla extract into a pan and bring to the boil. Whisk the egg yolk with the remaining sugar, flour, cornflour and make a crème pâtissière with the liquid. Cook until it is thick and creamy. Add the almond butter and hand blend until smooth and shiny. Season with Maldon salt. Transfer to a container and allow to set. Once set, knock back in a mixer until smooth and shiny.

For The Soufflé Mix

Preheat the oven to 180°C (fan).

Place a very small quantity of cherry compôte in the bottom of the moulds.

Make a medium peak French meringue with the sugar and egg whites. Incorporate the meringue into the knocked back soufflé base in 3 inclusions, without losing too much volume. Transfer to a piping bag and pipe into the soufflé moulds. Add a few slices of the confit cherries and flaked almonds so it resembles a bakewell tart. Bake for 8-9 minutes and dust with icing sugar before serving.

Chef's Tip

Don't put too much compôte in the bottom otherwise it prevents the soufflé from rising.

For The Almond Ice Cream (Prepare ahead)

Place everything, except the toasted almonds and Procrema, in a pan and bring to the boil. Cool quickly and, once it has reached 20°C, blend hard with the toasted almonds and Procrema until smooth.

Allow the mixture to 'mature' for 24 hours in the fridge. Blend until smooth, then transfer to either a Pacojet container or churn in an ice cream machine.

To Serve

Serve as pictured.

096
CSONS SHREWSBURY

8 Milk Street, Shrewsbury, Shropshire, SY1 1SZ

01743 272 709
www.csons-shrewsbury.co.uk Twitter: CsonsShrewsbury Instagram: csons_food
Facebook: CsonsShrewsbury

C SONS is a truly family affair.

"We are four brothers (SONS); Reuben, Adam, Ben and Josh, surname Crouch (C). Our passion for food has been with us since our early years when Dad's work took us all over the world and we experienced the excitement and diversity of global food and drink.

We've all followed our own journey through the world of food and CSONS is the culmination of over half a century of combined experience.

Our first venture opened in 2015 and the friendly cafe-restaurant in the heart of Shrewsbury serves breakfast, coffee, lunch, tea, cakes and dinner. Three years later we opened CSONS Ludlow as well. Being based in Shropshire we are surrounded by amazing growers and producers with whom we have built direct relationships. These close links with our suppliers means our menu changes on an almost daily basis in reaction to what is available and at its best. Our food is different; we use the best locally sourced produce and treat it with the respect it deserves by creating simple, unpretentious, globally inspired dishes that shout about the ingredients, reflect the seasons and are full of flavour.

Come and check us out, we're pretty confident you'll like what you find. We'd also like to meet you!" The CSons.

Locally sourced, globally inspired seasonal food and drink.

LABNEH, CUCUMBER, BEETROOT, COURGETTE, CHARD, HARISSA, TARKA OIL

SERVES 4

Enjoy with a glass of Shrewsbury born Paso Primero Somontano white wine, or even a cool, refreshing Love Cats Lager from Shrewsbury's Evolution Brewery.

Ingredients

Labneh

300g Greek yoghurt
5g salt
10ml lemon juice

Roast Beetroot

2 beetroot (peeled)
15ml olive oil
15ml balsamic vinegar
10g sugar

Harissa Roast Courgettes

2 courgettes
30g harissa
15ml olive oil

Vegetables

1 cucumber
250g rainbow chard
15g butter

Tarka Oil

1 bulb garlic
75ml rapeseed oil
5g fennel seeds
5g caraway seeds
5g cumin seeds

Method

For The Labneh (Prepare ahead)

Thoroughly mix the yoghurt, salt and lemon juice together, then strain through muslin overnight in the fridge.

For The Roast Beetroot

Preheat the oven to 180°C (fan).

Cut the beetroot into wedges. Toss with the olive oil, balsamic, sugar, salt and pepper to taste. Put in a roasting tray and roast for 20 minutes.

For The Harissa Roast Courgettes

Preheat the oven to 180°C (fan).

Cut the courgettes in half lengthways and divide each half into 3. Cover with harissa, olive oil, salt and pepper to taste. Place in a roasting tray and roast for 12 minutes.

For The Vegetables

Slice the cucumber in half across the middle, then each half lengthways, then in half lengthways again, but this time at an angle. Dry fry the cucumber in a non-stick pan on a medium to high heat until the flesh is charred. Remove and set aside.

Add the butter to the same pan, followed by the chard, season to taste and cook until wilted.

Chef's Tip

You can add a small amount of water to the pan to help steam the chard.

For The Tarka Oil

Peel the garlic and finely slice all the cloves. Put the rapeseed oil in a small pan, add the garlic and heat on a medium heat until the garlic begins to colour. Add the seeds and remove from the heat as soon as the garlic is browned.

To Serve

Start with the labneh as a base to the dish and layer with the cooked vegetables as pictured, finally drizzle with the tarka oil.

WILD BOAR, SWEETCORN, FENNEL, CABBAGE, BLACKBERRIES

SERVES 4

Enjoy with a glass of Shrewsbury born Paso Primero Somontano red wine or a Panting Partridge Perry from Leominster based Newton Court Cider.

Ingredients

Pickled Blackberries

30g sugar
90ml white wine vinegar
30ml fish sauce
150g blackberries

Blackberry Gravy

1 carrot (chopped)
1 onion (chopped)
4 cloves garlic (chopped)
20g ginger (chopped)
15ml olive oil
1 tbsp fresh marjoram leaves
200ml red wine
500ml beef stock

Creamed Sweetcorn

2 sweetcorn cobs
1 medium onion (finely diced)
25g butter
15ml olive oil
60ml double cream
3 sprigs fresh thyme (picked)
2½g paprika
1 red chilli (chopped)

Braised Fennel And Cabbage

1 bulb fennel
½ round summer cabbage
15ml olive oil
30ml white wine
5g fennel seeds

Wild Boar

4 wild boar leg steaks
salt and pepper
olive oil (drizzle of)
butter (knob of)

Method

For The Pickled Blackberries

Add the sugar, vinegar and fish sauce to a pan and heat until all the sugar is dissolved. Pour over the blackberries, cover and chill for at least 4 hours.

For The Blackberry Gravy

Add the carrot, onion, garlic and ginger to a hot pan with the olive oil. Fry until golden brown. *Deglaze* the pan with a little of the blackberry pickle *liquor,* then add the marjoram leaves and red wine. Boil until reduced by half. Pour in the beef stock and reduce until thick. Strain the blackberries, then add to the gravy. Set aside.

For The Creamed Sweetcorn

Remove the kernels from the cobs. Fry the onion in the melted butter and oil. Add the rest of the ingredients and simmer gently until the kernels are tender.

> **Chef's Tip**
>
> You can either leave the kernels whole or purée them with a blender. It's up to you!.

For The Braised Fennel And Cabbage

Preheat the oven to 180°C (fan).

Cut the fennel and cabbage into 4 wedges and place in an oven dish with the rest of the ingredients. Roast until tender and starting to brown.

For The Wild Boar

Season the boar steaks to taste and rub in a little olive oil. Fry in a heavy-based frying pan for a couple of minutes or until nicely browned. Flip, add the butter and baste for a couple of minutes. Remove and rest.

To Plate

Start with the sweetcorn, then add the braised cabbage and fennel. Slice a boar steak in half and place on top. Drizzle with the gravy and scatter a few blackberries around.

BLACKCURRANT JELLY, SPONGE, CUSTARD CREAM

SERVES 4

🍷 *Whinberry Gin Liqueur, Kirkwood Distillery, Shropshire (England)*

Ingredients

Blackcurrant Jelly

120g sugar
240ml water
400g blackcurrants
9g leaf gelatine (soaked in cold water)

Sponge

2 medium eggs
60g sugar
60g plain flour
25g butter (melted)
salt (pinch of)

Blackcurrant Compôte

60g sugar
water (splash of)
200g blackcurrants

Custard Cream

1 medium egg
1 yolk
45g sugar
525ml double cream
½ tsp vanilla extract

4 jelly moulds
15cm cake tin

Method

For The Blackcurrant Jelly

Boil the sugar and water together to dissolve the sugar, then add the fruit and simmer for 10 minutes. Remove from the heat and pass through a sieve; you should have 480ml of liquid. Stir the gelatine into the *liquor*, then pour into the jelly moulds.

For The Sponge

Preheat the oven to 160°C (fan).

Whisk the eggs and sugar until really thick and fluffy. Sieve in the flour and fold into the eggs. Add the melted butter and carefully fold it in. Transfer to the cake tin and bake for 15-20 minutes.

For The Blackcurrant Compôte

Dissolve the sugar in a splash of water, add half the blackcurrants and cook for 5 minutes until the liquid thickens slightly. Add the remaining blackcurrants, bring to boil, then remove from the heat.

For The Custard Cream

Whisk the eggs and sugar together lightly. Place 225ml of the double cream and the vanilla in a pan, bring to the boil, then pour over the eggs while whisking. Cook the custard over a *bain-marie* for about 10-15 minutes until thickened, then chill. Whip the remaining cream, then fold it into the cooled custard.

To Serve

Place a square of the sponge to one side of the plate, remove the jelly from the mould and place next to the sponge. Spoon a *quenelle* of the custard cream on top of the sponge and drizzle the compôte over the dish as pictured.

> **Chef's Tip**
>
> Use hot water to heat and clean the spoon between *quenelles* to help get the best shape and stop the cream sticking.

106
HARBORNE KITCHEN

175 High Street, Harborne, B17 9QE

0121 439 9150
www.harbornekitchen.com Twitter: @HarborneKitchen Facebook: Harborne Kitchen
Instagram: harbornekitchen

Harborne Kitchen was established in 2016 in an old butchers in Harborne, Birmingham, by chef Jamie Desogus. Taking inspiration from a variety of traditions, culinary practices and food producers, the restaurant is driven by a desire to create contemporary, playful, inviting and exciting cuisine.

The Chosen menu at Harborne Kitchen is a six or eight course tasting menu, curated to take the diner on a gustatory journey. Each of the dishes is carefully designed to provide layers of flavour, texture and pleasure, with the opportunity to discover enjoyment in the concept, in emotional satisfaction or in its sensory delights. Flavours, textures and ideas are woven through the experience, so that each dish is not only bold and delicious on its own, but makes connections across the whole meal.

Harborne Kitchen offers a relaxed experience of fine dining. While everything is done with care and precision, it is also a playful and invigorating experience. The food is bold, colourful and spectacular, where the comforts of traditional flavours and cuisines are enlivened by contemporary, creative ideas. The menu is a journey of discovery and delight for the diner; developing new ideas is a journey of discovery for the chefs.

FAMILY PORTRAIT...

BLUE PETER?

Jamie's Angels x

squad.

'You Swept?'

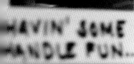

HAVIN' SOME HANDLE FUN...

MISE-EN!

clean Team

CRAIG, TOM + A KIWI

who's Taller?

GINGÉ

ROSH-HEY!

NOBODY PUTS JOE IN THE CORNER

A contemporary and spectacular restaurant and winner of the Good Food Guide's Best Local Restaurant in the Midlands award (2019).

CHICKEN LIVER PARFAIT, LICHFIELD STRAWBERRY, WHITE CHOCOLATE

SERVES 4-8

🍷 *Nyetimber N/V Demi-Sec, Sussex (England)*
Notes of golden apple, buttered pastry and fresh elderflower.

Ingredients

Chicken Liver Parfait

75ml Madeira
30ml brandy
75ml port
100g shallots (diced)
1 clove garlic (crushed)
400g chicken liver (presoaked in milk)
5 free-range eggs (room temperature)
400g unsalted butter (*clarified*)
20g pink salt

White Chocolate

175g white chocolate
45g medium to firm tofu

Strawberry Gel

500g class 2 strawberries
20g Minus 8 vinegar
6g agar agar (or 1g per 100ml liquid)

Chicken Skin And Oats

100g chicken skin
85g chicken fat
85g sugar
85g oats
15g salt
5 sprigs thyme (picked)

To Serve

Lichfield strawberries
freshly ground black pepper
Minus 8 vinegar

terrine mould (lined)

Chef's Comments

This dish was voted in the Top 10 Dishes of 2019 by the Good Food Guide. All elements from this dish can be made a day ahead.

Method

For The Chicken Liver Parfait

Preheat the oven to 110°C (fan).

Reduce the Madeira, brandy and port with the shallots and garlic until reduced by half.

Blitz the livers (no milk) with the reduction in a blender until smooth. Add 1 egg at a time, blending for 5 minutes until smooth. Add the melted butter, a little at a time, while still blending slowly. Season with pink salt.

Pass the mixture through a fine sieve into the mould and cover with foil. Place into a deep oven tray and fill with warm water until two-thirds of the way up the terrine. Cover the oven tray with foil too.

Cook for 45 minutes and, using a temperature probe, check the temperature has reached above 70°C for a minimum of 2 minutes. Cool the terrine in an ice bath in the fridge; it is important to chill the terrine within 90 minutes.

For The White Chocolate

While the parfait is cooking, heat the chocolate in a *bain-marie*, then transfer to small blender and blend with the tofu, season to taste. Transfer to a piping bag and set aside.

For The Strawberry Gel

Steep the strawberries and vinegar under vacuum at 80°C in a water bath for 2 hours. Alternatively, use a mixing bowl and *bain marie*. Drain the liquid, bring to the boil and add the agar agar. Whisk and bring to the boil, then transfer to a suitable container. Once set, blend the mixture, then pass through a fine sieve.

Note: The strawberries are a by-product but can be kept and used; we add them to the kitchen team's porridge for breakfast! Just bear in mind that most of the flavour has been transferred to the liquid.

For The Chicken Skin And Oats

Preheat the oven to 180°C (fan).

Scrape and remove the tough fat from the underside of the skin, then place the skins on baking trays. Bake for 25 minutes or until crispy. Chop, then set aside.

Preheat the oven to 95°C (fan).

Combine the remaining ingredients and bake in the oven for 2 hours or until a crunchy texture is achieved.

Combine the chopped chicken skin and crunchy oats to make the topping.

To Serve

Serve as pictured.

GOOSNARGH DUCK, SAND GROWN CARROT, STAR ANISE, ORANGE

SERVES 4

🍷 *Barbera D'Alba, GD Vajra, Piedmont (Italy)*
Notes of hedgerow, plums and dried spices and herbs.

Ingredients

Sauce

3 banana shallots (thinly sliced)
20ml white wine vinegar
100ml white wine
100ml orange juice
500ml roast duck or chicken stock (we make ours but this can be bought)
2 star anise
2 sprigs thyme

Carrot Purée

8 carrots (peeled, thinly sliced) (we use sand carrots but a good quality organic carrot will be great)
250g butter
10ml white wine vinegar

Gastrique

200g sugar
250ml white wine vinegar
1 star anise

Goosnargh Duck

1 large duck breast (pre-scored)
2 sand carrots (or good quality organic, peeled)
butter (for basting)

Method

For The Sauce

Sweat the shallots until translucent in a wide, heavy-based pan. Add the vinegar and wine and reduce until a syrup is formed. Add the orange juice and reduce until syrupy. Pour in the stock and reduce by half. Once the desired consistency is achieved, remove from the heat and add the star anise and thyme sprigs.

For The Carrot Purée

Place the sliced carrots in a wide, heavy-based pan with the butter and vinegar. Cover the pan with a lid so no air or moisture can escape and cook very quickly until tender. Blitz in a blender and pass through a fine sieve. Reheat gently when ready to serve.

For The Gastrique (Prepare ahead)

Reduce all the ingredients until a soft caramel is formed. Set aside.

For The Duck

Preheat the oven to 180°C (fan).

Render the duck, skin-side down, in a medium pan. Control the temperature to not scorch the skin and tip away any fat so you don't 'deep fry' the breast. Once the fat has rendered, turn the duck over and seal the base. Turn the duck onto a cold oven tray and place in the oven for 2 minutes, then turn the duck over for a further 1 minute. Let the duck rest for 4 minutes.

Chef's Tip

We buy whole Goosnargh ducks that have been salt-aged by our butcher, but we encourage you to use a local butcher; it will be more cost effective to buy breast only. Remove the duck from the fridge at least 1 hour before cooking.

To Serve

Cook the whole carrots for 8 minutes in a rolling, foaming butter, basting regularly. Gently reheat the sauce and the carrot purée. Carve the rested duck and serve immediately, drizzled with the gastrique.

We serve this dish with a duck fat and sesame focaccia bread.

WILDFLOWER HONEY PARFAIT, SORREL SORBET, LAVENDER GASTRIQUE

SERVES 4-8

 Coteaux du Layon, Domaine Ogereau, Loire Valley (France). Notes of honey and sticky peach.

Ingredients

Wildflower Honey Parfait

100g sugar
150g egg yolk
100g wildflower honey
15g gelatine (soaked in cold water)
500ml double cream (semi-whipped)
salt (to taste)

Sorrel Sorbet

50g sorrel leaf
130ml water
50g yoghurt
15g sugar
20g glucose

Lavender Gastrique

400g sugar
300ml white wine vinegar
5 sprigs lavender

Honeycomb

2 tbsp glucose
400g sugar
100g honey
2 tsp bicarbonate of soda

Milk Crisp

1 litre whole milk
80g glucose

Garnish

lavender flowers (optional)
cut comb honey (optional)

Method

For The Wildflower Honey Parfait

Heat the sugar with enough water for it to dissolve. When the sugar reaches 110°C, start whisking the egg yolks in a mixer. Once the sugar has reached 121°C, add the mixture to the eggs slowly and beat until the mixture has slightly chilled. Gently heat the honey and stir in the gelatine until dissolved. Once fully dissolved, incorporate this into the egg mix. Add the salt to the semi-whipped cream and fold into the mixture. Transfer to a lined suitable container and freeze.

For The Sorrel Sorbet

Blend together all the ingredients on high power until the sorrel has completely broken down. Working quickly, add this to an ice cream machine and churn until silky smooth. Freeze.

For The Lavender Gastrique

Combine the sugar and vinegar and bring to a steady boil. Once the mixture turns to a light caramel, remove from the heat, add the lavender and allow to cool. Pass through a fine sieve to remove the lavender. Once cool, the gastrique should be runny enough to dress a plate but firm enough to not seep.

For The Honeycomb

Heat the glucose, sugar and honey to 145°C. Add the bicarb and whisk. Pour onto a silicone mat and allow to cool.

For The Milk Crisp (Prepare ahead)

Bring the glucose and milk to a gentle heat. Blend using a hand blender to create a foam, then spoon the bubbles onto a silicone mat. Dehydrate in the oven at 70°C for 8 hours.

> **Chef's Tip**
>
> Don't forget to season the parfait. It makes the difference. The gastrique adds real balance to the dish and cuts through the sweetness.

To Serve

Serve as pictured. In the restaurant we serve this with cut comb honey and lavender picked from the HK garden.

THE KING'S HEAD

21 Bearley Road, Aston Cantlow, Henley-in-Arden, Warwickshire, B95 6HY

01789 488 242

www.thekh.co.uk Instagram: khastoncantlow Facebook: The King's Head - Aston Cantlow

The King's Head is a traditional 15th Century village inn located in picturesque Aston Cantlow in the heart of Warwickshire, approximately six miles from Stratford-upon-Avon.

Flanked by a huge chestnut tree, the Grade II listed building oozes charm and character, from its impressive black and white timbered Tudor exterior and, internally, its low beams, polished flagstones and crackling log fires.

The building and area are steeped in history, including the church next door where Shakespeare's parents married. They are rumoured to have held their wedding breakfast in The King's Head. The King's Head still caters for celebrations and weddings of all sizes.

There are many walks that start and end at The King's Head and children and dogs are welcome (dogs are allowed in the bar).

The King's Head is open all day, every day and diners can choose to eat from light snacks to a full à la carte menu, or pub classics. Food can also be served in the shade of the chestnut tree in the beer garden. The mouthwatering Sunday roasts are particularly popular.

Wherever guests choose to eat, they are guaranteed delicious, freshly prepared, locally sourced food, some of which even comes from their own kitchen garden.

The food is matched by an excellent selection of wines, quality draught beers and cask ales. Open daily, The King's Head is the ideal place in which to unwind and relax.

The King's Head photography by Paul Matthews, PJM Productions

Superb surroundings, friendly faces and a relaxed environment; this is the perfect place in which to unwind and enjoy quality food and drink.

SALAD OF CRAB, WASABI CREME FRAICHE, PICKLED CUCUMBER, RADISH

SERVES 4

Estola Verdejo Bodegas Ayuso la Mancha (Spain)
Tropical fruit flavours, fresh and crisp.

Ingredients

Wasabi Crème Fraîche

100g crème fraîche
1 tsp wasabi paste

Salad Of Crab

200g picked white crab meat
5g coriander (chopped)
5g red chilli (finely diced)
salt (pinch of)

Pickling Liquor

100g caster sugar
100ml water
100ml white vinegar
10 pink peppercorns

Vegetables

½ cucumber
2 radishes

Garnish

2g micro coriander cress (or smallest you can find)
12 cucumber flowers
5g pickled pink ginger

blow torch

Method

For The Wasabi Crème Fraîche

Mix the ingredients together until well combined.

For The Salad Of Crab

Mix all the ingredients into the wasabi crème fraîche.

For The Pickling Liquor

Mix all the ingredients together and bring to the boil on a low heat. Let the mixture cool.

For The Vegetables

Peel the cucumber skin into ribbons. Slice the inside into thin strips lengthways and blow torch to add colour. Cut each strip into several pieces diagonally. Add the cucumber ribbons to the pickling *liquor* for about 15 minutes, then drain, reserving the *liquor*.

Ribbon the radishes with a peeler and place in iced water.

Chef's Tip

The *liquor* can be drained from the cucumber and kept for a few weeks to pickle other vegetables.

To Serve

Place the crab meat mixture into a ring, then add the cucumber ribbons, radish and sliced cucumber. Place the ginger on top and garnish with the coriander and cucumber flowers.

PAN FRIED LOIN OF VENISON, FETA MASH, KING'S HEAD GARDEN BEETROOT

SERVES 4

🍷 *Primitivo Terre Avare 2017 (Italy)*
Intense sweet aromas, full and velvety.

Ingredients

Venison Jus

1kg (approx) venison bones (ask your butcher to cut these for you)
1 carrot (diced)
1 onion (diced)
2 sticks celery (diced)
water (to cover)
½ bottle red wine
2 sprigs thyme

Venison

4 x 140g venison loins
oil (drizzle of)
salt and pepper

Baby Beetroot

2 red beetroot
2 golden beetroot
2 rainbow beetroot (or smallest that you can find)

Feta Mash

300g Maris Piper potatoes (peeled)
50ml double cream
50g butter
200g feta cheese (grated)
20ml whole milk
salt
pepper

To Serve

20g broad beans (warmed in boiling water)

Method

For The Venison Jus

Preheat the oven to 180°C.

Roast the bones for about 40 minutes until brown, then place them into a large pan.

Place the vegetables into the roasting tin and roast until golden, then add to the pan with the bones. Cover with water and bring to the boil. Simmer for 4 hours, then drain the stock and set aside.

Place the red wine and thyme into a pan and simmer on a low heat until reduced. Add the stock to the reduced red wine. Simmer until the jus coats the back of a spoon. Strain before serving.

For The Venison

Seal the venison loins in a hot pan with oil, salt and pepper for approximately 4 minutes each side until golden. Remove and allow to rest.

> **Chef's Tip**
> Always allow meat to rest. Once cooked, place on a tray in a warm place to allow the meat to relax; this will make the meat tender.

For The Baby Beetroot

Boil the baby beetroots in separate pans, peel, then halve or quarter them.

For The Feta Mash

Boil the potatoes until soft, then drain and mash them.

Gently warm the cream and butter in a pan, add the grated feta and milk and blend well. Stir into the mashed potatoes, season, then transfer to a piping bag and keep warm.

To Serve

Pipe the feta mash into the middle of the plate with a further 3 dots around the edge. Slice the loin into 5, add the beetroot and broad beans. Finish with the jus.

APPLE TARTE TATIN, VANILLA ICE CREAM

SERVES 4

Muscat Beaumes de Venise, Domaine de Durban 2014 (France). Rich, fruity, clean but not too sweet.

Ingredients

Apple Tarte Tatin

1 pack pre-rolled puff pastry
100g *clarified butter*
4 Granny Smith apples (cored)
80g caster sugar
30ml water
80g apricot jam

Vanilla Ice Cream

75g sugar
3 egg yolks
500ml double cream
1 vanilla pod (scraped)

Garnish

4 slices apple (reserved)
flour (to dust)
oil (to deep fry)
caster sugar (to sprinkle)

Method

For The Apple Tarte Tatin

Using a 15cm saucer as a template, cut out 4 circles of the puff pastry. Pierce each circle of pastry with a fork, leaving a 2cm gap around the edge. Refrigerate on greaseproof paper for 20 minutes.

Clarify the butter by melting it, then using the top half when it has separated.

Thinly slice the apples on a mandoline, keeping 4 slices to one side for later.

Place the sliced apples in a fan shape around the pastry, leaving a thumbnail gap at the edge. Use a pastry brush to cover the apples with the *clarified butter*. Dust with sugar and return to the fridge to set. Repeat the butter and sugar stages 2 more times returning to the fridge each time.

Preheat the oven to 180°C.

Bake the tartes in the oven for 15-20 minutes until golden.

Place the water and the jam in a pan and melt to use as a glaze; keep the mixture warm.

Brush the hot tartes with the glaze.

Chef's Tip

Life is too short to make puff pastry so shop bought is fine; the pre-rolled sheets work better.

For The Vanilla Ice Cream

Whisk together the sugar and yolks until thick and creamy.

Warm the cream slowly with the vanilla seeds until boiling point, then remove from the heat and add to the egg mix, whisking continuously. Pour into a clean pan and stir over a low heat until the mixture thickens enough to coat the back of a spoon. Place in the fridge until cold, then churn in an ice cream machine. Freeze until ready to serve.

To Finish And Serve

Lightly flour the 4 slices of apple and deep fry until golden. Sprinkle with caster sugar and serve as pictured.

THE LION + PHEASANT

49-50 Wyle Cop, Shrewsbury, SY1 1XJ

01743 770 345
www.lionandpheasant.co.uk Twitter: @LionandPheasant Facebook: lion.and.pheasant

Originally built in the 16th Century, this beautiful townhouse in the heart of Shrewsbury combines unique charm and original features with cool fresh interiors.

The former coaching inn, renovated in 2010, is a unique combination of historic quality and contemporary design. As a 2 AA Rosette restaurant and three-star hotel awarded by the AA since 2011, it is the perfect destination for an evening out in the à la carte restaurant or an overnight stay in the hotel. Each of the Lion + Pheasant's 22 bedrooms is individually styled, combining the best of contemporary design with the historic inn.

The restaurant is featured in the Michelin Guide, Good Pub Guide and described as 'one of a kind' with its unique oak beamed Tudor interior. It has established itself as a great destination and is ranked as one of the top dining destinations in Shrewsbury.

The kitchen brigade led by head chef Paul Downes creates outstanding, innovative, seasonal menus, maintaining the quality of the dishes by using locally sourced suppliers in and around Shrewsbury.

Paul has 19 years of experience and it shows with the quality and high standard in the menus he produces. A local born and bred, his relationships with the local producers are unrivalled. Not only does Paul put his modern twist on classic dishes but he also takes inspiration from unique and unusual flavours from around the world.

As chef Paul Downes says, "the joy is not in cooking for yourself, the joy is in cooking for others". It is clear that the whole brigade follows this motto. They pour their hearts and souls into ensuring every mouthful is perfectly balanced and full of flavour.

NORI CURED SALMON, BEETROOT TEXTURES, DILL OIL, WASABI CREAM

SERVES 8

Grillo Vitese (Sicily)
Spicy wine with stone fruit and ginger. Refreshing lime note on the finish.

Ingredients

Nori Cured Salmon

1 side salmon (skin removed)
300g caster sugar
300g table salt
12 sheets nori (blend 6 sheets to a powder)

Beetroot Textures

1 medium golden beetroot
2 medium purple beetroot
1 candy beetroot (peeled)

Dill Oil

100g fresh dill
100ml rapeseed oil

Wasabi Cream

200ml cream (semi-whipped)
wasabi paste (to taste)

Garnish

50g wasabi peas (lightly crushed)

Method

Chef's Tip

This dish is best prepared a day in advance.

For The Nori Cured Salmon (Prepare ahead)

Slice the salmon into 4 slices lengthways, starting at the tail end.

Combine the sugar and salt. Lay the salmon slices in a tray, then pour the sugar and salt mixture over the top, cover the tray with cling film and chill for 3 hours. Wash the salmon in cold water, then pat dry. Put the salmon into a tray and dust with the nori powder, rolling until covered.

Lay out 2 overlapping sheets of cling film. Place the 6 remaining sheets of nori on top, overlapping them to slightly longer than the salmon. Soften the nori using a clean, damp sponge.

Lay the salmon on the nori, alternating head to tail with the first 2 strips, then do the opposite with the remaining 2 strips.

Using the cling film, roll the salmon over carefully to wrap in the nori, then roll tightly, tie the ends and chill overnight.

For The Beetroot Textures

Preheat the oven to 180°C (fan).

Bake the golden and purple beetroot for 1½ hours. Once cooked, peel the beets, keeping the colours separate. Purée the purple beets in a food processor until smooth. Cut the golden beetroot into ½cm dice.

Thinly slice the candy beetroot then, using a cutter, cut out rings.

For The Dill Oil

Blend the dill and oil to a vibrant green oil, then pass through a fine sieve.

For The Wasabi Cream

Mix the wasabi paste into the cream to taste, then whip fully.

To Serve

Serve as pictured.

SHROPSHIRE LAMB, LOIN, RACK, BELLY & FAGGOT, ROSEMARY POMMES ANNA, ASPARAGUS, COURGETTE & BASIL PUREE

SERVES 4

Aglianico (Italy)
Aromas of cherry and raspberry on the nose and a full-bodied, well balanced palate.

Ingredients

Rosemary Pommes Anna

250g butter (melted)
2 sprigs rosemary (chopped)
8 large potatoes (peeled, thinly sliced on a mandoline)
salt and pepper

Lamb

1 lamb belly (bones removed)
1 litre lamb stock
2 x 4 bone lamb racks
1 lamb loin
50g butter

Lamb Faggots

200g lamb mince
1 lamb kidney (roughly chopped)
cumin (large pinch of)
salt (pinch of)
caul fat

Courgette Purée

6 courgettes (peeled, skins reserved)
75ml water
150g basil

To Serve

asparagus (trimmed)
girolles (*sautéed*)

terrine mould

Method

For The Rosemary Pommes Anna (Prepare the day before)

Preheat the oven to 180°C (fan).

Combine the butter and rosemary.

Fill a terrine mould with layers of potato, seasoning and brushing with rosemary butter, until all are used. Cover with foil and bake for 30 minutes. Remove the foil and bake for a further 10 minutes. Cool slightly, cover with greaseproof paper, then press with a heavy weight overnight in the fridge.

For The Lamb Belly

Roll and tie the belly, then lightly seal off in a hot pan. Cover with stock and slowly braise for 3 hours.

Remove the belly from the stock onto a tray to cool. Once cold, slice into portions.

Pass the cooking *liquor* through a sieve, then chill. Once cold, remove and discard the fat, then reduce the *liquor* by half over a high heat.

For The Lamb Faggot

Combine the mince and kidney, season with salt and cumin. Shape into 4 balls and wrap with caul fat.

For The Courgette Purée

Roughly chop the white of the courgette, then *sauté* until translucent. Add in the green skins and water and gently heat until just softening. Blend in a food processor, with the basil, until smooth.

To Serve And Assemble

Preheat the oven to 180°C (fan).

Sear the lamb racks, skin-side down, in a large pan. Once crisp, turn over and sear on all sides. Remove from the pan onto a tray with the faggots and place in the oven for 10-15 minutes.

Sear the loin and belly in a pan on all sides, add the butter and baste.

Blanch the asparagus in salted water for 2 minutes.

Assemble as pictured.

Chef's Tip

Ask your butcher to *French trim* your lamb racks, trim the fat off your lamb loin and debone your lamb belly.

ICED VANILLA PARFAIT, RHUBARB TEXTURES, OAT CRUMBLE, RHUBARB SORBET

SERVES 4

Essensia Orange Muscat, California (USA)
Vibrant orange, this wine delivers sweet oranges and apricots on the palate.

Ingredients

Iced Vanilla Parfait

55g caster sugar
20ml water
40g egg yolk
250ml double cream (semi-whipped)
15g vanilla bean paste

Rhubarb Sorbet

125g caster sugar
150ml water
50ml grenadine
200g rhubarb (peeled, chopped)
15g glucose

Oat Crumble

40g oats
75g plain flour
60g caster sugar
60g unsalted butter
10g golden syrup

Rhubarb Textures

10 large sticks rhubarb
250ml grenadine

Garnish

micro red vein sorrel
viola flowers

2½cm x 7½cm moulds for parfait
lined baking tray

Method

Chef's Tip

For best results, prepare this dish a couple of days in advance.

For The Iced Vanilla Parfait (Prepare ahead)

Combine the sugar and water in a pan and heat until it reaches 121°C.

Whip the yolk in a mixer, then slowly pour on the hot sugar mixture. Cool slightly, then fold into the semi-whipped cream and add in the vanilla bean paste. Pour the mixture into lined moulds and freeze overnight.

For The Rhubarb Sorbet

Bring all the ingredients to the boil in a pan, then reduce the heat to a gentle simmer and cook until the rhubarb is just softening. Blend until smooth, pass through a fine sieve and chill for 1 hour. Churn in an ice cream machine and freeze.

For The Oat Crumble

Preheat the oven to 140°C (fan).

Mix all the dry ingredients together with the butter to breadcrumb stage. Add the syrup and mix again. Sprinkle the mixture onto a lined baking tray and cook for 10-15 minutes until golden, stirring halfway through. Set aside to cool. Store in an airtight container.

For The Rhubarb Textures

Peel the rhubarb, cut the tops and bottoms off and discard. Cut into 15cm pieces, place in a pan and cover with the grenadine. Heat gently until the rhubarb starts to soften, then remove half the rhubarb and chill. Continue to cook the remaining rhubarb until just cooked, then blend until smooth.

To Serve

Serve as pictured.

136
THE OYSTER CLUB

43 Temple Street, Birmingham, B2 5DP

0121 643 6070
www.the-oyster-club.co.uk

I n the heart of Birmingham city centre on Temple Street, The Oyster Club is a relaxed, seafood-focussed restaurant and oyster bar, by Adam Stokes (of Michelin-starred Adam's), that opened in April 2019. Boasting a stylish interior, with an air of luxury - yet feeling equally relaxed. Interior inspiration is drawn from the sea with subtle nods to the ocean, and lights inspired by pearls, shell-like seating, and even subtle fish scales on the exterior sign.

The seafood-led menu is centred around the highest quality seafood from the UK and further afield. The focus is on simple dishes done perfectly, and you can enjoy everything from Teriyaki salmon, to whole roasted Dover sole.

Whether you book a table to celebrate a special occasion or pop in after work for a glass of wine and a few small plates at the bar, The Oyster Club caters for every occasion.

Dining options include small plates, fish plates and large plates, giving you the opportunity to tailor your own dining experience. Oysters occupy a prominent place on the menu, with four or five beautiful varieties available from across the UK and France.

To accompany the delicious seafood dishes, there is a stunning wine list, sourced from around the globe. If wines aren't your thing, they also have a collection of small production spirits and cocktails, including their signature Oyster Club Martini.

THE
OYSTER CLUB   2018
BY ADAM STOKES

EST. _The_ 2018

OYSTER CLUB

BY ADAM STOKES

A great place to enjoy delicious food and drinks in a great atmosphere.

TEMPURA OYSTERS, PICKLED KOHLRABI, WASABI DIP

SERVES 4

 Blanc de Blancs, Hattingley Valley, 2013, Hampshire (England)

Ingredients

12 good quality fresh rock oysters

Pickled Kohlrabi

250ml chardonnay vinegar
250ml water
40g caster sugar
¼ shallot (sliced)
¼ lemon
½ tsp black peppercorns
½ tsp white peppercorns
1 kohlrabi
½ red chilli (deseeded, finely diced)
½ green chilli (deseeded, finely diced)

Wasabi Dip

2 egg yolks
1 tbsp Dijon mustard
250ml sunflower oil
salt (pinch of)
2 tbsp lime juice
wasabi paste (to taste)
sriracha (to taste)

Tempura Batter

200g cornflour
200g plain flour
25g baking powder
20g salt
sparkling water (as required)
1 lime (zest of)
chives (finely chopped)

To Serve

oil (for deep frying)
1 lime (zest and juice of)
rock salt

Method

For The Pickled Kohlrabi

Combine the vinegar, water, sugar, sliced shallot, lemon and peppercorns in a pan. Bring to 65°C, then leave to infuse. When cooled to room temperature, strain.

Thinly slice the kohlrabi and chop into ribbons. Cover the ribbons with the pickle *liquor* and leave for 3-4 hours. Finally, mix through the finely chopped chillies.

For The Wasabi Dip

Place the egg yolks and Dijon mustard in a bowl. Gradually drizzle in the sunflower oil whilst whisking all the time (don't add it too fast or it will split!). Once the mayonnaise is thick, stir in the salt, lime juice, wasabi and sriracha to your desired heat. Optional: you can transfer the dip to a mousse syphon gun and add 2 charges. Shake well before use.

For The Tempura Batter

Combine the cornflour, plain flour, baking powder and salt. Once mixed, add in the sparkling water until the batter is just thick so that it will coat your oysters nicely. Stir in the lime zest and add the finely chopped chives.

To Finish

Heat a deep fat fryer to 180°C. Open the oysters and place in a bowl. Clean the shells for serving. Strain off any liquid, then add a generous squeeze of lime juice. Next, coat the oysters in flour then add to the herby batter and gently place in the fryer for around 3 minutes until golden and crispy.

Using a microplane or fine grater, zest a lime over the top of the oysters. Top each oyster with a small pinch of the pickled kohlrabi. Transfer the oysters back to the cleaned shells and serve in a bowl of rock salt, with the wasabi dip on the side.

SEA BASS CEVICHE, MOOLI, LIME YOGHURT, GINGER VINAIGRETTE

SERVES 4

Junmai Ginjo Sparkling Sake, Akashi-Tai (Japan)

Ingredients

Lime Yoghurt

300g Greek yoghurt
2 limes (zest and juice of)
salt (pinch of)

Ginger Vinaigrette

250g mooli
50g ginger
150ml light soy sauce
150ml rice wine vinegar
150ml mirin

Coriander Oil

200ml sunflower oil
1 bunch coriander
sea salt (a good pinch of)

Sea Bass Ceviche And Mooli

1 mooli
salt (pinch of)
1 x 600g sea bass
1 lime

Garnish

coriander (small bunch of)
lime (zest of)

Method

For The Lime Yoghurt

Combine the yoghurt with the zest and juice of the limes, then season with salt to taste. Transfer to a piping bag.

For The Ginger Vinaigrette

Blend or finely grate the mooli and ginger and strain off any excess liquid.

Bring the soy sauce, rice wine vinegar and mirin to the boil, then pour it over the mooli and ginger, mix well. Once cool, strain off some of the liquid and set aside. This will be used to marinate the sea bass. Save the mooli and ginger mix, this will be used in the dish as well.

For The Coriander Oil

Warm the oil to just above room temperature.

Place the coriander and salt in a blender. Slowly add in the oil until well blended and it is a vibrant green colour. Put the oil mixture into a fine sieve and leave to drain for a couple of hours. Discard the sieve contents and transfer the oil to a squeezy bottle.

For The Sea Bass Ceviche And Mooli

Cut the mooli into small cubes and season with salt.

Skin the sea bass and remove the head and tail. Finely slice the sea bass fillet and use the liquid from the mooli and ginger vinaigrette to dress the fish. Add in a good squeeze of lime juice, leave for around 2 minutes to marinate and for the flavour to be absorbed into the fish.

To Serve

Neatly lay the slices of sea bass on a plate and dress with the raw mooli cubes, small blobs of the mooli and ginger mixture, dots of lime yoghurt and some fresh coriander leaves.
Finally, finish with some lime zest over the top and a drizzle of coriander oil all over the dish.

COD, ROASTED CRAB SAUCE, FENNEL, CHARRED HISPI CABBAGE

SERVES 4

Châteauneuf-du-Pape Blanc 2017, Domaine
Chante Cigale, Rhône (France)

Ingredients

Roasted Crab Sauce

1kg crab shells
2 carrots (roughly chopped)
2 sticks celery (roughly chopped)
1 bulb fennel (roughly chopped)
2 banana shallots (roughly chopped)
3 cloves garlic (roughly chopped)
vegetable oil (drizzle of)
1 tsp fennel seeds
1 star anise
1 tbsp tomato paste
1kg cherry tomatoes (roughly chopped)
150ml brandy
250ml Madeira
350ml white wine
3 litres chicken stock
1 lemon (juice of)
salt (to taste)

Fennel

1 large bulb fennel
1 lemon (squeeze of)
olive oil (drizzle of)
sea salt

Hispi Cabbage

1 Hispi cabbage
oil (drizzle of)
salt

Cod

1 cod fillet (skin removed, cut into
4 x 120g portions)
sea salt
olive oil (drizzle of)
1 lemon (juice of)

Method

For The Roasted Crab Sauce

Preheat the oven to 180°C.

Roast the crab shells on a tray in the oven for around 20 minutes.

Colour the vegetables and garlic in a heavy-based pan with the oil. Once coloured, add in the fennel seeds, star anise and tomato paste, and continue to cook on a medium heat for 2 minutes. Stir in the tomatoes and cook for 10 minutes. Add the roasted crab shells, brandy, Madeira and wine, bring to a rapid boil and reduce by half. Add the stock and bring to the boil. Reduce by half until you get a deep crab flavour. Pass the reduced liquid through a fine sieve and season generously with lemon juice and salt.

For The Fennel

Thinly slice the fennel on a mandoline to get thin ribbons.

Mix the fennel with a drizzle of olive oil and a good squeeze of lemon juice, then season with sea salt. Slowly warm the fennel in a pan to soften slightly.

For The Hispi Cabbage

Trim the outer leaves and discard. Cut the inner leaves into quarters and *blanch* in boiling water for 2 minutes until slightly softened. Cool immediately in iced water.

When ready to serve, char the cabbage in a hot frying pan with a little oil so that it gains some colour and a roasted flavour. Season with salt.

For The Cod

Preheat the oven to 180°C.

Season the cod with salt. Place the cod portions in a hot, non-stick frying pan with a little olive oil and colour one side of the fish so that it's a lovely golden colour. Transfer to the oven for around 3-4 minutes until the cod is just cooked. Finish with a generous squeeze of lemon.

To Serve

Place a pile of fennel in the middle of each plate for the cod to sit on. Top the cod with the charred cabbage and pour a generous amount of sauce all around the fish.

146
PURECRAFT BAR & KITCHEN

30 Waterloo Street, Birmingham, B2 5TJ

0121 237 5666
www.purecraftbars.com Twitter: purecraftbars Facebook: purecraftbars

Established in 2014 by Paul Halsey, of Purity Brewing Company and Andreas Antona, of renowned Michelin-starred restaurants The Cross in Kenilworth and Simpsons of Edgbaston, their idea was simple. To bring together real home cooked food with great beer and relaxed yet exceptional service.

The stripped back, open plan bar and restaurant, set in a Victorian office space, is devoted to delivering interesting craft beers and beautiful, mouthwatering food. Their aim is to perfectly match beer with food at every opportunity, although people who aren't huge fans of beer certainly won't be disappointed by what's on offer.

The Purecraft cellar bar and tasting room are available for private events and functions and they pride themselves on tailoring to individual needs.

Five years on and they're still delivering 'best in class' English food matched with world class beer and great hospitality to all who visit the heart of the Birmingham business district. Whether you're popping in for beer battered fish and chips, or the famous smoked pork and cider Scotch eggs, you won't be disappointed. Everything is done to make sure it's the best you'll have.

Established in 2014 in the heart of Birmingham business district, the idea was simple; to bring together great beer and real food in an inclusive and welcoming environment.

SMOKED PORK SCOTCH EGG, MUSTARD MAYO

SERVES 4

Purity Cider
(England)

Ingredients

Scotch Egg

6 large free-range eggs
300g smoked sausagemeat
100g plain flour
200g panko breadcrumbs
salt (to season)

Mustard Mayo

good quality mayonnaise
Coleman's English Mustard

Method

For The Scotch Egg

Bring a large pan of salted water to a gentle simmer. Carefully add 4 of the eggs and cook for 6 minutes (this will give you a runny yolk). Immediately refresh the eggs in iced water. Once completely cold, take care to peel the eggs without breaking them - they will be quite soft!

Split the sausagemeat into 4 x 75g balls. Place the meat between 2 sheets of cling film and press them down to form a flat circle. Remove the top sheet of cling film and place a soft boiled egg in the centre of each sausage 'patty'. Gently wrap the meat around the egg. Place in the fridge for at least 30 minutes to firm up.

Prepare the *pane*. Whisk the remaining eggs and place into a bowl. In separate bowls, place the flour and the panko. Coat each Scotch egg in the flour, then the whisked egg and finally the panko. Place back in the fridge to firm up.

Set a deep fat fryer and fan oven to 180°C. Deep fry the Scotch eggs until golden brown, then place onto a tray, and transfer to the oven for 6 minutes.

Chef's Tip

Sit the eggs in a bowl of warm water for a few minutes before boiling them - this will reduce the stress on the shells and hopefully stop them from cracking!

For The Mustard Mayo

Mix the mayonnaise and mustard together. You can do whatever ratio you prefer, or even go with just the mustard!

To Finish And Serve

Remove the Scotch eggs from the oven and season all over with salt. Leave to rest for 1-2 minutes before serving with the mustard mayo.

LAWLESS BATTERED HADDOCK, CHIPS, MUSHY PEAS, TARTARE SAUCE

SERVES 4

*Purity Lawless Lager
(England)*

Ingredients

Chips

2 litres beef dripping or vegetable oil
2kg Maris Piper potatoes (cleaned)

Tartare Sauce

200g good quality mayonnaise
50g capers
50g cornichons (thinly sliced)
50g shallots (diced)
1 tbsp dill (chopped)

Lawless Batter

200g self-raising flour
100g rice flour
5g sea salt
turmeric (pinch of)
500ml Purity Lawless lager (chilled)

Haddock

4 x 200g haddock fillets
200g plain flour

To Serve

1 tin mushy peas
1 lemon (cut into 4 wedges)
sea salt (to season)
malt vinegar

Method

For The Chips

Fill a deep fat fryer with the beef dripping or vegetable oil and heat to 180°C. Cut the Maris Pipers into 10mm thick chips (I prefer to keep the skin on). Wash the chips under cold, running water until the starch has been removed. Drain, pat dry, then fry for 3 minutes.

For The Tartare Sauce

Combine all of the ingredients well.

For The Lawless Batter

Sieve the dry ingredients together and gradually whisk in the Purity Lawless lager taking care not to overmix - a few lumps are fine.

> **Chef's Tip**
>
> Make sure your Lawless lager is very cold before making the batter, it will make all the difference!

To Finish And Serve

Heat the mushy peas in a pan and keep warm.

Dredge the haddock in the flour, then coat with the batter. Gently lower the fish into the fryer and cook for 5-6 minutes, turning halfway through - you may have to do this in batches depending on the size of your fryer. Remove and allow to rest on a kitchen cloth.

Deep fry the chips for another 3-4 minutes (check to make sure they are cooked through). Drain and season with salt.

Place a generous spoonful of mushy peas onto each plate and place the fish on top. Season with sea salt and malt vinegar. Top with a lemon wedge. Divide the chips between the 4 plates and serve with the tartare sauce.

CARAMALT BURNT CUSTARD

SERVES 4

 Purity Maravilla Sour Beer
(England)

Ingredients

Caramalt Burnt Custard

50g caramalt grains (whole, not crushed)
375ml double cream
125ml whole milk
80g egg yolk
110g caster sugar
100g Demerara sugar

4 shallow crème brûlée dishes
blow torch

Method

To Make The Caramalt Burnt Custard

Preheat the oven to 175°C (fan).

Place the caramalt grains onto a tray and roast for 5 minutes. This will intensify the aroma and add more flavour to the custard.

Pour the double cream, milk and roasted grains into a saucepan. Place on a medium heat and bring to the boil. Remove from the heat and allow to infuse for 30 minutes.

Preheat the oven to 100°C (fan).

Gently whisk together the egg yolk and caster sugar, taking care not to incorporate too much air. Pass the cream through a fine sieve into the egg mixture and combine. Allow the mix to stand for a few minutes before skimming off any foam.

Place the 4 shallow crème brûlée dishes onto a flat tray and pour the mixture into the dishes. Carefully transfer to the oven and cook for 30 minutes, or until the custards are firm with only a very slight wobble. Remove from the oven and allow to cool before placing in the fridge to set.

When the custard is cold and completely set, remove them from the fridge. If any condensation has formed on the surface, place a sheet of kitchen paper on top to remove it. Cover the surface of the custards with the Demerara sugar and tip off any excess. Use a blow torch to caramelise the sugar - taking care not to burn them! Allow the sugar to cool and set before serving.

To Serve

Serve as pictured.

> **Chef's Tip**
>
> Use a blow torch to remove any bubbles from the surface of the custards before cooking.
>
> Caramalt grains are easy to find online however if you are struggling, just pop in for a beer and ask the chefs for some!

156
PURNELL'S RESTAURANT

55 Cornwall Street, Birmingham, B3 2DH

0121 212 9799
www.purnellsrestaurant.com Twitter: @purnellsrest Instagram: purnellsrestaurant

f there's one man who can reasonably lay claim to kick-starting the Midlands' gastronomic revolution, it's Glynn Purnell.

The Yummy Brummie moved like a whirlwind through the Second City at the start of the Millennium, winning a first Michelin star for a place that was once derided by critics.

Having worked with Andreas Antona at Simpsons, in Kenilworth, and Claude Bosi, at Hibiscus, in Ludlow, and having completed stages at various Michelin-starred restaurants in France and with Gordon Ramsay in London, he decided to go it alone.

Purnell launched Jessica's in Birmingham's red light district, securing a Michelin star for food that dazzled an expectant nation and earned plaudits from such three-star chefs as Ramsay and Heston Blumenthal.

He relocated to the city centre, opening his eponymous restaurant and securing a new Michelin star in January 2009. Located in one of Birmingham city centre's finest conservation areas, close to Colmore Row and St Phillips Cathedral, Purnell's was established by its chef patron in July 2007.

The 45-cover restaurant occupies a Victorian redbrick and terracotta corner building, with large windows on both sides providing plenty of natural light during the day.

The restaurant has its own bar and lounge area for diners only, where a pre-dinner cocktail or after dinner coffee or digestif can be enjoyed in comfortable surroundings.

Glynn Purnell's bold and innovative cooking provides the ultimate gourmet adventures and has brought him critical acclaim and numerous awards, not to mention regular slots on Saturday Kitchen and The Great British Menu, on which he was twice a winner.

The restaurant accommodates tables of up to six diners. The private dining room is available for parties of up to 12 diners. And the food is cooked by the original Yummy Brummie and his team.

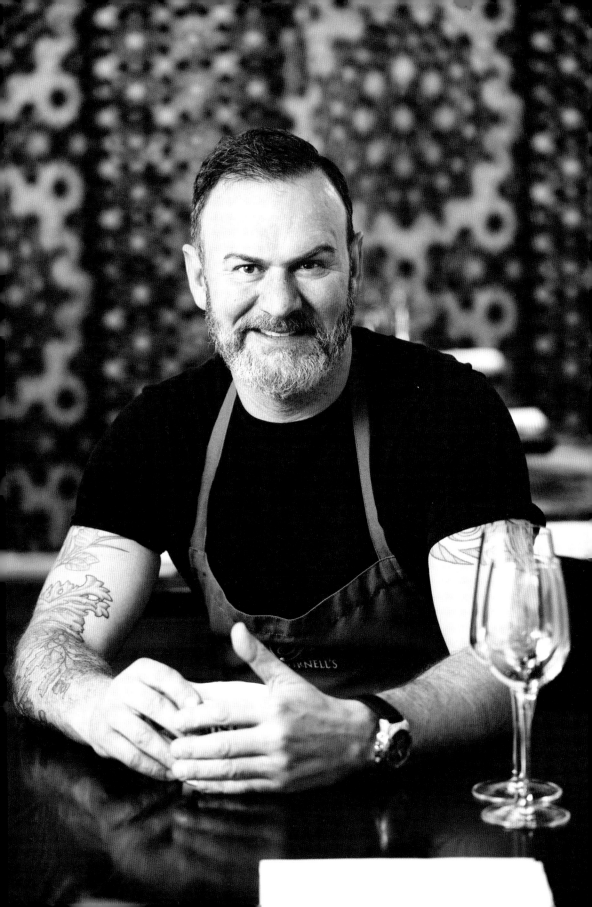

"In my restaurant, I like people to laugh and enjoy the food. I like the food presentation to be flamboyant, colourful, romantic, funny... it should be like a rollercoaster when you're eating it. This ethos defines the plates served at Purnell's." Glynn Purnell.

DUCK, SPICED PLUM JAM, WATERCRESS

SERVES 4

Cabernet Sauvignon, Art Series, Leeuwin Estate, 2013, Margaret River (Australia)

Ingredients

Duck

2 heads pak choi
3 duck breasts
salt and freshly ground black pepper

Spiced Plum Jam

200g caster sugar
200ml white wine vinegar
1 medium chilli (chopped)
chilli powder (pinch of)
2 cloves garlic (sliced)
lime juice (squeeze of)
soy sauce (splash of)
6 plums (stoned, chopped)
1 tbsp chopped coriander
salt and ground ginger

Garnish

watercress (bunch of)

Method

For The Duck

Preheat the oven to 180°C.

Break the pak choi into individual leaves, then split each leaf down its length. Set aside.

Prepare the duck breasts by removing any sinew from the underside of the breast. Using a very sharp knife, score the skin with a series of slashes, being careful not to go too deeply and cut into the flesh.

Heat a frying pan over a medium heat, add the breasts, skin-side down, and cook for about 3 minutes until the skin has caramelised. Pour off the excess fat and reserve.

Lay the duck breasts, skin-side down, in a roasting tin and place in the oven for 7-8 minutes. Remove from the oven and leave to rest for 10 minutes.

Pour the reserved fat and any fat in the roasting tin back into the frying pan and set over a medium heat. Once hot, add the pak choi and toss in the hot duck fat. Remove from the pan and season with salt and black pepper.

For The Spiced Plum Jam

Heat the sugar and vinegar in a saucepan, stirring until the sugar has dissolved, then cook until the mixture starts to thicken. Add the chilli and chilli powder, garlic, lime juice and soy sauce, then stir in the plums and cook for 20-30 minutes until tender. Add the coriander, then remove the pan from the heat and season with salt and ground ginger.

To Serve

Carve the duck into slices and divide between 4 plates. Serve with the pak choi and plum jam, garnished with watercress.

Chef's Comment

Big, juicy, spicy plums! Oo-er missus! They're exactly what you need to cut through the rich duck. The crisp pak choi blends and adds balance. Duck is a fab meat either spiced up or classically served. Fat and delicious!

MONKFISH MASALA, RED LENTILS, PICKLED CARROTS, COCONUT

SERVES 4

 Viognier, Domaine Gerovassiliou, 2018, Macedonia (Greece)

Ingredients

Pickled Carrots

3 carrots (peeled, *julienne*)
1 tbsp fenugreek seeds
1 tsp ajwain seeds
1 tsp black mustard seeds
½ tsp onion seeds
1 tsp cumin seeds
⅓ tsp chilli flakes
1 tsp salt
vegetable oil (enough to cover the carrots)

Monkfish Masala

300g rock salt
4 x 130g monkfish fillets
4 tbsp masala spice mix
25g butter

Red Lentils

vegetable oil (splash of)
½ onion (peeled, chopped)
1 tbsp mild curry powder
225g dried red lentils
500ml chicken stock
½ red chilli (finely chopped)
2 heaped tbsp chopped coriander
½ lime (juice of)
salt

Coconut Garnish

400ml can full-fat coconut milk
1 kaffir lime leaf
salt (pinch of)
½ fresh coconut (flesh only, thinly sliced into strips on a mandoline)

Garnish

coriander shoots (sprouted coriander seeds)

Method

Chef's Comment

Who doesn't like monkfish? It's meaty in a delicate fish form, but it's big and can hold itself too. Next question - who doesn't like curry? Monkfish and curry - two of my favourites together. This dish works as a starter or as the main event. The lentils, using vegetable stock, can work as a vegetarian option.

For The Pickled Carrots (Prepare up to 2 weeks ahead)

Preheat the oven to 90°C.

Spread the carrots out on a baking tray and put in the oven overnight, or for 8 hours, until dried out. Pack the carrots into a sterilised, airtight jar.

Mix all the spices and salt with enough vegetable oil to cover the carrots. Pour the oil over the carrots in the jar and seal. Leave for a couple of weeks (longer if you can) in a cool place.

For The Monkfish Masala (Prepare ahead, allow 24 hours)

Sprinkle the salt over the monkfish and leave for 5-6 minutes to draw out the moisture. Rinse the salt off thoroughly under cold running water. Wrap the monkfish in a clean tea towel and leave overnight in the fridge.

Spread out the spice mix on a plate and coat the monkfish. Seal each fillet in a vac pack bag and cook for 11 minutes in a water bath at 63°C. Alternatively, wrap each fillet in heatproof cling film. Heat a saucepan of water until it reaches 63°C, add the wrapped fillets and cook for 11 minutes, keeping the temperature constant.

Melt the butter in a frying pan over a medium heat until foaming. Remove the fish from the bags or cling film, then sear on each side for 2-3 minutes until golden brown and crisp all over.

For The Red Lentils

Heat the oil in a saucepan and sweat the onion over a gentle heat for 4-5 minutes until softened. Stir in the curry powder, then add the lentils, stir well and cover with stock. Simmer for 10-15 minutes, or until the lentils are tender.

When the lentils are cooked, stir in the chilli, coriander and lime juice and season to taste with salt. Set aside.

For The Coconut Garnish

Simmer the coconut milk with the lime leaf and salt over a medium heat for 15-20 minutes until reduced by half.

Heat a frying pan until hot and toast the coconut strips for about 2 minutes until golden brown and fragrant.

To Serve

Serve as pictured.

BURNT ENGLISH CUSTARD EGG SURPRISE, MARINATED STRAWBERRIES, TARRAGON, BLACK PEPPER HONEYCOMB

SERVES 8

 Banyuls, 2014, Gérard Bertrand (France)

Ingredients

Black Pepper Honeycomb

200g caster sugar
35g honey (preferably Solihull Heather)
70g liquid glucose
2 tbsp water
10g bicarbonate of soda
freshly ground black pepper

Marinated Strawberries

150g caster sugar
150ml Banyuls (sweet red wine)
50ml water
3 star anise
½ bunch tarragon
6-7 strawberries per person (hulled, halved if large)

Caramel

70g caster sugar
2 tbsp water
sunflower oil (for greasing)

Burnt English Custard

9 large free-range eggs
85g caster sugar
500ml double cream
2 vanilla pods (scraped)

Garnish

tarragon (small bunch of, deep fried in vegetable oil until crisp)

greased, non-stick baking tray
blow torch

Method

For The Black Pepper Honeycomb

Bring the sugar, honey, glucose and water to the boil in a saucepan. Place a sugar thermometer in the pan and boil the mixture until it reaches 150°C, then add the bicarbonate of soda and quickly whisk to combine. The mixture will rise up when the bicarb is added, so be careful. Immediately pour the mixture into a non-stick baking tray. Add several grindings of black pepper and leave to set for about 1 hour at room temperature, uncovered. Once set, break into shards.

Chef's Tip

The honeycomb mixture will double in volume, so make sure you have a big enough pan.

For The Marinated Strawberries

Combine all the ingredients, except the strawberries, in a saucepan and gently simmer until the liquid has reduced by half. Pour over the strawberries in a small bowl and leave to infuse for 30 minutes.

For The Caramel

Heat the sugar and water in a heavy-based saucepan over a medium heat until the sugar has dissolved, then increase the heat slightly and bring to the boil. Every now and then, brush the sides of the pan with a pastry brush dipped in cold water to prevent sugar crystals forming. Boil for about 3-4 minutes, to a dark golden-brown caramel.

Pour the caramel into a greased, non-stick baking tray and leave to cool for about 1 hour at room temperature, uncovered. Once set, shatter into small shards.

For The Burnt English Custard

Remove the tops of the eggs and separate the yolks and whites. Remove the membrane from the shells, then clean and dry them. Whisk the egg yolks and sugar in a bowl until pale and fluffy. Gently heat the cream with the vanilla seeds and pods in a small pan to just below boiling point. Remove from the heat, discard the pods and pour the hot cream over the egg yolk mixture, whisk until combined. Pour the mixture into a clean pan, return to a gentle heat and stir until it starts to thicken enough to coat the back of a spoon. Set aside and leave to cool slightly.

To Serve

Carefully spoon or pipe the custard mixture into the cleaned eggshells and put in an empty egg box to keep them level. Sprinkle a little caramel over the custard in each egg and melt using a kitchen blow torch. Serve as pictured.

166
THE RIVERSIDE AT AYMESTREY

Aymestrey, Herefordshire, HR6 9ST

01568 708 440
www.riversideaymestrey.co.uk Twitter: TheRivKitchen Facebook: riversideinnaymestrey

The Riverside at Aymestrey is a country inn and pub that aims to showcase and promote the best of the region, with their unique food and sustainable ethos.

The Riverside at Aymestrey is situated deep in the heart of the Herefordshire countryside, just on the southern edge of the Mortimer Forest, yet still close to Ludlow and Hereford. Authentic and atmospheric, the 16th Century black and white building is surrounded by the natural beauty of the River Lugg valley, great to relax alongside in the summer months or next to the log fires in the bar in the winter. The inn has nine bedrooms, all recently renovated to create a cosy feeling, including three garden rooms offering a unique escape within the landscaped grounds.

Winning several accolades for sustainability and their work with local artisan suppliers, including Visit England Best Tourism Pub 2018, Herefordshire Sustainable Business Award and Herefordshire Best Food and Drink Business for dedication to using produce from the surrounding region, not only in its food producers, but also drinks, arts and craft.

Their rural Herefordshire project includes extensive organic kitchen gardens, an orchard, beehives and wild meadows from where they forage. The delicious menus include rabbit, trout, fruit, nuts and herbs all sourced from within metres of the restaurant.

"Our aim is to create a sustainable, rural escape where you can experience the best of the surrounding region through its landscape, the food and the atmosphere we offer." Andy Link, chef patron.

LAMB SWEETBREADS, SWEETCORN, BACON, HERBS

SERVES 4

Paso-Vermú with Chase Gin - A great way to start a meal; a classic sweet vermouth with a Paso-Primero twist. It's crafted from a blend of Paso-Primero Tinto and Blanco which is sweetened, fortified and infused with Pyrenean herbs and spices.

Ingredients

Sweetcorn Purée

500g sweetcorn kernels
100g butter
150ml double cream

Panna Cotta

250g sweetcorn purée
600ml double cream
200ml whole milk
8 leaves gelatine (soaked in cold water)

Sweetbreads

12 small lamb sweetbreads (we prefer the testicles for this dish)
whole milk (for soaking)
extra virgin rapeseed oil (drizzle of)
butter (large knob of)
1 sprig rosemary
Maldon sea salt
freshly cracked pepper

To Serve

fresh seasonal wild or homegrown herbs
herb oil
locally smoked bacon (thinly sliced, fried until extra crispy)

Method

For The Sweetcorn Purée

Cook the sweetcorn in the butter and cream until soft. Blend until smooth, then pass through a fine *chinois*.

For The Panna Cotta

Heat the sweetcorn purée with the milk and cream, then season to taste. Stir the bloomed gelatine into the mixture, then pour into moulds and refrigerate for a minimum of 4 hours.

For The Sweetbreads

Soak the sweetbreads in milk for 2-3 hours, then drain well. Pan fry in oil until golden brown on both sides, reduce the heat and add the butter and herbs. Baste with butter until cooked through, then season.

> **Chef's Tip**
>
> Use only the freshest and best quality lamb for this dish, although simple the quality is in the ingredients. Using local cream and butter and a rare breed organic smoked bacon will make all the difference.

To Serve

Spoon some of the leftover sweetcorn purée on the plate. Place the panna cotta and sweetbreads on the plate and dress with foraged herbs, herb oil and crispy bacon.

SHROPSHIRE ORGANIC CHICKEN, BARLEY, CARROT, WILD MUSHROOM

SERVES 4

Local organic cider, something with a traditional and apple flavour. Matching with what you use in the sauce should tie in with the dish nicely.

Ingredients

Sauce
chicken bones (ask your local butcher for these)
3 onions (chopped)
4 cloves garlic (chopped)
3 sticks celery (chopped)
3 mushrooms (chopped)
80g malt grains or toasted barley
1 sprig thyme, 1 sprig rosemary
3-4 bay leaves, 1 tbsp malt extract
350ml local, organic cider (we use Newton Court Leominster)
50ml cider vinegar (we use Willy's cider vinegar by Chase, Herefordshire)

Barley
6 cloves garlic (chopped)
2 onions (chopped), 2 bay leaves
rapeseed oil (drizzle of)
1 sprig thyme, 1 sprig rosemary
150g pearl barley
2 tbsp honey (we used honey from our own hive)
350ml water
sauce (ladleful of)

Chicken
4 chicken supremes
4 tbsp Bennett & Dunn rapeseed oil
4 tbsp butter
dried hay (small handful of)

Carrot Purée
8 organic or home-grown carrots (peeled, chopped)
60g butter, 15ml hazelnut oil

To Serve
8-10 seasonal, wild mushrooms (yellow chanterelles work best)
seasonal, wild herbs (yarrow, hairy bittercress and dandelion leaves in this recipe)

Method

For The Sauce (Prepare ahead)
Preheat the oven to 180°C.

Roast the bones in a roasting pan for 40 minutes.

Fry the onions, garlic, mushrooms and celery until browned. Stir in the barley and fry off. Add the roasted bones and herbs, then cover in water. Simmer for 6 hours until it is light brown in colour and has a good flavour.

In a separate pan, reduce the cider and vinegar by two-thirds, add to the chicken stock, then pass through a sieve. Reduce to desired consistency, then finish with the malt extract. Taste for seasoning.

For The Barley
Lightly fry off the garlic, onions and bay in the rapeseed oil with the thyme and rosemary. Add the barley and honey. Cook out with a ladle of the sauce and the water. Simmer gently until soft, add more water if required.

For The Chicken
Preheat the oven to 190°C.

Fry the breasts in an ovenproof pan in a splash of oil, making sure that they are sealed on all sides. Add the butter, then position the hay around the chicken. Igniting the hay, cover with foil before placing the pan in the oven and roasting for 25-35 minutes or until cooked. Smoking in this manner can be difficult at home (especially where smoke alarms are involved!). Stove top smokers are available. Alternatively, use an outside BBQ for a few minutes before using the oven to finish.

> **Chef's Tip**
>
> With all meats resting is vital. We also cook the chicken with its wing bone and skin on; it keeps the breast more succulent as it rests.

For The Carrot Purée
Place the carrots in a pan and cover them with water. Cook until soft, about 10-15 minutes, then drain. Blend with the butter and hazelnut oil until smooth. Season to taste.

To Serve
Lightly fry the wild mushrooms. Spoon the carrot purée and cooked barley onto a plate. Slice the chicken and place in the centre. Toss the foraged herbs in warm meat juices and serve with the sauce.

STOUT PARFAIT, GINGER ICE CREAM, BROWN BREAD CRUMB

SERVES 4

Coffee... Hundred House Coffee is an amazing artisan roaster in the Shropshire hills. With a dish this sweet and rich, a delicious coffee complements it perfectly.

Ingredients

Brown Bread Crumb

4 slices good quality rye or wholemeal bread
50g brown sugar
2 oranges (zest of)

Stout Parfait

400g soft brown sugar
200ml good quality local stout
6 large egg yolks
2 leaves gelatine (soaked in cold water)
250ml double cream (whipped lightly)

Ginger Ice Cream

568ml whole milk
568ml double cream
60g ginger in syrup
350g sugar
10 large egg yolks

4 individual parfait moulds

Method

For The Brown Bread Crumb

Preheat the oven to 180°C.

Blitz the bread, sugar and orange zest. Bake for 10-20 minutes until dry and crispy. Allow to cool, then blitz to a powder.

For The Stout Parfait

Boil the stout and brown sugar to 120°C.

Whisk the egg yolks until pale and fluffy, then pour the hot syrup carefully and gradually over the eggs while still whisking. Add the softened gelatine to the hot mix. Fold through the whipped cream. Freeze until set in individual moulds.

Chef's Tip

Use a stout with a great flavour, something you enjoy to drink. We use Wye Valley Stout, just because of its malty depth of flavour.

For The Ginger Ice Cream

Heat the milk, cream and ginger in a pan to a simmer.

Whisk the egg yolks and sugar until pale and light. Pour over the cream and milk mix, then whisk back into the pan and cook, whilst whisking, until it thickens. Churn in an ice cream machine.

To Serve

Serve as pictured.

176
SALT

8 Church Street, Stratford-upon-Avon, Warwickshire, CV37 6HB

01789 263 566
www.salt-restaurant.co.uk Twitter: @salt_dining Facebook: saltstratford Instagram: salt_dining

Chef patron Paul Foster enjoyed an epic year in 2018. He won his first Michelin star, published his debut book, Salt, and swept all before him by winning a number of awards.

"It was a crazy, crazy year," he says. "Becoming the first chef to win a Michelin star for Stratford-upon-Avon was the highlight."

Now he's keen to build on that success as he strives for ever higher standards at a restaurant that's built on the use of exceptional ingredients.

Paul trained under Sat Bains, in Nottingham, before becoming head chef at Tuddenham Mill and then at Mallory Court. After that, it was time to go it alone. He successfully launched a Kickstarter campaign, bought his own restaurant and, in short order, achieved the near-impossible with the ultimate recognition from Michelin.

"It's all down to working with great producers and having the drive and determination to push on," says Paul. "We like to keep things simple and work with people who do the right thing. So we have a great relationship with a local flour mill, we work with a guy who I rate as the world's best butter maker and we get our beef from a wagyu farm out in Suffolk.

"It's all about respecting the ingredients and using the best possible produce when it's in peak condition."

Paul credits his family for helping him to succeed; from a mother who let him bake cakes for bouncers as a kid, to a loving wife who's with him every step of the way. And he's looking to push on in years to come to make sure 2018 was just the beginning.

salt

relaxed fine dining

Salt; a fine dining restaurant using the best produce, served in a relaxed atmosphere where you can sit back, relax and enjoy your dining experience.

CARROT COOKED IN CHICKEN FAT, CRISPY CHICKEN SKIN, PICKLED CARROT

SERVES 4

🍷 *Gewurztraminer, Gocke, Alsace, 2017
(France)*

Ingredients

Chicken Fat

1kg chicken skin
250g butter

Crispy Chicken Skin

chicken skin from 4 breasts
sea salt

Chicken Sauce

500ml dry white wine
1 litre brown chicken stock (reduced by half)

Carrots

4 donkey carrots
100g butter
5 sprigs thyme
10g salt

Pickled Carrots

8 purple baby carrots
400ml vinegar
100g sugar
100ml water

Croutons

2 slices seeded bread
50g butter

To Finish

4 mixed colour baby carrots
20g sorrel leaves
20 nasturtium leaves

Kilner jar

Method

For The Chicken Fat

Gently cook the skin in the butter, in a heavy-based pan, so the fat is lightly foaming. Stir regularly and cook for 1½ hours until the skin is golden and crispy. Pass through a fine sieve whilst still warm. Set in the fridge.

For The Crispy Chicken Skin

Preheat the oven to 170°C.

On a chopping board, scrape the fat and any excess meat from the inside of the chicken skin. Stretch the skin over a wire rack outside up and season with sea salt. Put the wire rack over a baking tray and cook for 15 minutes. It should be golden and crisp. Store in an airtight container until needed.

For The Chicken Sauce

Reduce the wine down to a glaze, add the chicken stock and reduce to a slightly thin sauce-like consistency.

For The Carrots

Peel the carrots keeping a nice barrel shape. Place in a vac pack bag with the rest of the ingredients and seal tightly. Once sealed, cook in a water bath at 90°C for 2 hours, they should be soft but still retain a little bit of texture. Chill in iced water to stop the cooking.

For The Pickled Carrots

Place all the ingredients in a Kilner jar, ensuring the carrots are submerged and seal tightly. Put the jar in a water bath and heat to 63°C, leave for 3 hours and allow the jar to cool before opening.

For The Croutons

Tear the bread into rough croutons, taking care not to squash it. *Sauté* in foaming butter until golden brown, drain on kitchen paper and cool.

To Finish

Preheat the oven to 180°C.

Portion the cooked carrot into 5cm barrels and roast in the oven with a large spoon of the chicken fat for 6-8 minutes, basting regularly. Remove the carrot and place into the bowl with 2 spoons of the fat, warm the chicken sauce and add 2 spoons to the bowl so it separates with the fat. Shave the raw carrot, cut the pickled carrots lengthways into 4 and arrange on the plate. Chop the chicken skin and sprinkle over the carrot. Add the croutons and finish with the sorrel and nasturtium leaves.

SERVES 4

Potato Terrine

250g butter, 5 sprigs thyme
5 large Maris Piper potatoes (peeled, sliced 1mm thick on a mandoline)
salt

Watercress Velouté

1 banana shallot (peeled, sliced)
1 clove garlic (crushed)
20g butter
100ml double cream
200ml chicken stock
250g watercress
100g parsley

Chervil Tubers

8 small chervil tubers (peeled, tops removed, well washed), 100g butter

Partridge Sauce

6 partridge carcasses (chopped)
8 cloves garlic (crushed)
150g butter
300ml dry white wine
100ml dry sherry
10 sprigs thyme
2 banana shallots (peeled, cut into quarters)
750ml reduced chicken stock

Partridge

2 whole partridges (heads, food sacks and entrails removed)
salt (to season), 50g butter
200ml partridge sauce

To Finish

fresh watercress

terrine mould (lined with cling film)

For The Potato Terrine (Allow 24 hours)

Preheat the oven to 160°C.

Gently melt the butter with the thyme, allow to infuse. Line a terrine mould with cling film and brush the bottom with the butter. Place a layer of potato across the bottom, brush with the butter and season with salt. Continue this process until the potato is 1cm above the top of the mould, but only season alternate layers as you build it. Wrap excess cling over the top of the potatoes and cover with a lid or tin foil. Bake for 45-50 minutes or until a knife goes easily through the centre. When cooked, press in the fridge with another terrine mould on top and around 2kg of weight. Leave overnight.

For The Watercress Velouté

Sweat the shallot and garlic in the butter. Pour in the cream and stock and bring to the boil.

Add the watercress and parsley and cook for 30 seconds. Blend until completely smooth. Pass through a fine sieve into a bowl set over ice.

For The Chervil Tubers

Blanch in boiling, salted water for 4 minutes, then leave to cool on a wire rack.

For The Partridge Sauce

Roast the carcasses and garlic in butter until golden. Drain the butter, then pat the bones and pan dry. Return the bones and garlic to the pan and *deglaze* with the alcohols. Reduce by three-quarters, then add the remaining ingredients. Bring to the boil, cover and simmer for about 30 minutes until a sauce consistency. Season, then pass through a fine sieve and muslin cloth.

For The Partridge

Preheat the oven to 180°C.

Remove the wishbone with a sharp knife. Cut around the leg just above the foot, trim off all the claws but the middle one. Season, then colour all over in a hot pan with the butter. Place on their backs, then cook in the oven for 4 minutes. Rest for 8 minutes. Cut off the legs, remove the thigh bone and trim the legs. Glaze the legs in boiling partridge sauce.

To Finish

Remove the breasts from the bone and crisp up the skin in a hot pan. Caramelise the chervil tubers in foaming butter until golden brown. Cut 1cm slices of the terrine and pan fry both sides in hot oil to crisp and colour. Warm the velouté and serve as pictured. Finish with watercress and the partridge sauce.

BRITISH STRAWBERRIES, ELDERFLOWER, AERATED WHITE CHOCOLATE, STRAWBERRY SORBET

SERVES 4

 Pineau des Charentes, Vieux, Domaine de Landon, (France)

Ingredients

20 British strawberries (topped)

Lacto Fermented Strawberry Purée

1kg strawberries (hulled)
200g whey

Strawberry Sorbet

1kg lacto fermented strawberry purée
100g sugar
100g pro sorbet

Elderflower Syrup

2 limes
10 heads elderflower
50g citric acid
1 litre water
500g caster sugar

Caramelised White Chocolate Crisp

200g white chocolate

Aerated White Chocolate

500g white chocolate
30g sunflower oil

Garnish

1 purple elderflower head

isi gun and 2 canisters

Method

For The Lacto Fermented Strawberry Purée (Prepare ahead)

Mix the strawberries with the whey. Vac pack tightly and leave in a warm room at around 28°C for 48 hours. Remove from the bag and blend until smooth.

For The Strawberry Sorbet

Whisk the ingredients together well and taste to check the flavour and sugar levels. Freeze in Pacojet containers until solid. Churn in the Pacojet before needed to check the consistency. Alternatively, churn in an ice cream machine.

For The Elderflower Syrup (Prepare ahead)

Slice the limes into 5 or 6 round slices. Place into a large container with the elderflower and citric acid. Mix the water and sugar together and bring to the boil, pour over the elderflower and leave to cool. Cover with a tight-fitting lid and keep in the fridge for 12 hours. Pass the syrup though a muslin cloth and store in the fridge until needed.

For The Caramelised White Chocolate Crisp

Preheat the oven to 180°C.

Spread the chocolate out evenly on a lined baking sheet and bake for a few minutes until lightly golden. Place in a blender and blend to a smooth golden purée. Roll out to 2mm thickness between 2 sheets of parchment paper and set in the fridge.

For The Aerated White Chocolate

Melt the chocolate with the oil and pour into an isi gas canister, charge with 2 gas chargers and shake well. Keep warm until needed. Turn the canister upright and squirt into a lined plastic vacuum container about 1-2 cm high. Place the lid on and set to vacuum. Place the container into a vac pack machine and close the lid to remove the air. Carefully watch the white chocolate rise as the air is removed and press stop when the chocolate is around 5cm high. Place the whole container in the fridge for 2 hours to completely set.

To Serve

Dress the strawberries with elderflower syrup, leave to *macerate* for 5 minutes. Cut the aerated white chocolate into small blocks and snap the white chocolate crisp into small shards. Arrange on a plate and finish with a scoop of the sorbet. Sprinkle with purple elderflowers.

186
SIMPSONS

20 Highfield Road, Birmingham, B15 3DU

0121 454 3434
www.simpsonsrestaurant.co.uk Twitter: simpsons_rest
Instagram: simpsons_restaurant Facebook: simpsonsrestaurant

Nearly 20 years have passed since Simpsons in the leafy Birmingham suburb of Edgbaston gained its first Michelin star.

Two decades of excellence. Two decades of evolution. Two decades during which Simpsons has earned its reputation as a Midlands powerhouse of gastronomy.

The food served at Simpsons has always been inventive, responding to their discerning diners' desire for new and exciting dishes.

But their innovation is underpinned by respect for the past - by a grasp of culinary tradition.

Expect the finest seasonal ingredients treated with respect, imagination and skill.

Expect modern British cuisine of the highest order - beautifully-crafted and cleverly-conceived dishes that delight all the senses.

Chef patron is Andreas Antona, who has a wealth of experience and knowledge gained by working in fantastic kitchens all over Europe.

His right-hand man is Luke Tipping, who was awarded the first ever Midlands Chef of the Year Award and is a Professorship of Culinary Arts at the renowned University College Birmingham.

Alongside them work a brigade of passionate and highly-skilled young chefs.

An equally dedicated and knowledgeable front-of-house team, led by general manager Gianluca Austin-Rizzo ensures that Simpsons customers feel pampered and cosseted.

Simpsons is a place dedicated to the highest standards, but utterly relaxed.

The slick, contemporary decor, which respects the elegance of the Georgian mansion in which Simpsons is housed, adds to the sense of luxury.

Likewise the beautiful garden, where guests can sit and relax before and after lunch or dinner.

Escape and enjoy!

The team at Simpsons - Birmingham's first Michelin-starred restaurant and a winner of multiple awards - continues to set the very highest standards and delights its guests with exciting food and fantastic service.

BEETROOT, ICED GOAT'S CHEESE, WASABI

SERVES 4

 Agiorgitiko Rosé, Ktima Driopi, 2018 (Greece)

Ingredients

Beetroot Purée

300g large red beetroots (peeled, root removed)
460ml water
90g caster sugar
460ml cider vinegar

Vinaigrette

100ml rapeseed oil
25ml Champagne or white wine vinegar
salt

Baby Beetroots

4 baby candy beetroots
4 baby golden beetroots
4 baby red beetroots
3 litres water
3 cloves garlic
3 tbsp sugar
3 tbsp salt
12 sprigs thyme

Iced Goat's Cheese

1 log Innes Goats cheese (Tamworth)

Wasabi Mayonnaise

200g mayonnaise
1 x 43g tube wasabi paste
salt and pepper

Wasabi Nuts

50g wasabi nuts

Garnish

mixed edible flowers
sorrel

Method

For The Beetroot Purée

Grate the beets on the widest setting on a box grater. Place in a pan with all the other ingredients, bring to the boil, reduce to a simmer and stir occasionally until all the liquid has been absorbed and the beetroot is tender. Place into a food processor and blend until smooth. Pass through a sieve, then chill.

> **Chef's Tip**
>
> Rather than making the beetroot purée, you could use shop bought jars of pickled beetroot. Strain off and reserve the liquid. Blend the beetroots in a food processor with enough liquid to create a smooth purée.

For The Vinaigrette

Whisk the ingredients together in a bowl until *emulsified*, season to taste.

For The Baby Beetroots

Place the different colour beetroots in separate pans and top with just enough water to cover. Crush the garlic cloves with the back of a knife. To each pan, add a clove of garlic, 4 sprigs of thyme and a tablespoon of salt and sugar. Bring to the boil, then turn down to a rolling simmer, cooking until the beetroots are tender and a knife can be inserted to the middle with no resistance.

Remove from the pans and rub with kitchen paper to remove the skins. The skins should come off easily. Whilst still warm, dress with the vinaigrette and allow to cool.

For The Iced Goat's Cheese (Prepare ahead)

Remove the rind from the cheese. Crumble into small pieces by hand and place on a lined baking sheet in the freezer overnight. Transfer to a food bag and crush with a rolling pin until all the pieces are small and even in size. Reserve in the freezer in an airtight container.

For The Wasabi Mayonnaise

Place the mayonnaise and wasabi into a bowl and whisk until combined. Season to taste and reserve in a piping bag in the fridge.

For The Wasabi Nuts

Place the nuts into a food bag and crush with a rolling pin to form a powder like consistency.

To Serve

Serve as pictured.

CHICKEN, MUSHROOMS, ASPARAGUS, SHERRY VINEGAR SAUCE

SERVES 4

 *Pinot Noir, Sauska, 2013
(Hungary)*

Ingredients

Chicken

1 large Cotswold white chicken (Caldecott Farm)
1 litre water (warm)
100g salt

Chicken Sauce

chicken wings
chicken drumsticks
200g shallots (sliced)
2 plum tomatoes (diced)
80ml sherry or white wine vinegar
2 cloves garlic, 5g thyme
reserved chicken stock, 20g butter

Pomme Purée

900g Maris Piper potatoes (washed, baked)
80ml double cream (warm)
80ml whole milk (warm)
160g unsalted butter (melted)

Black Garlic Purée

500g black garlic (soaked in cold water)
300ml water

Onion Crumb

1 large white onion (peeled, quartered)
salt
pepper

Hen Of The Woods

1 punnet hen of the woods mushrooms
(*sautéed* in oil and butter until foaming)

Green Asparagus

4 spears green asparagus (*blanched*, brushed
with rapeseed oil)

White Asparagus

4 spears white asparagus (woody ends removed)
whole milk
salt, sugar

Method

For The Chicken

Dissolve the salt in the water, then chill in the fridge.

Remove the wings and reserve for the sauce. Remove the legs, cutting as close to the backbone as possible. Split the legs into thighs and drumsticks, reserve the drumsticks for the sauce. Remove the excess bone from the chicken carcass, leaving just the crown.

Place the thighs and back spine in a pan and just cover with cold water. Bring to the boil, then simmer for 1 hour, skimming off any scum. Strain and reserve the stock for the sauce.

Place the chicken crown into the brine for 1 hour. Rinse off, then pat dry.

Preheat the oven to 80°C (fan).

Roast the crown for 1½ hours or until the core temperature has reached 65°C. Brown the skin in a hot pan until golden brown. Remove the breasts, slicing from the sternum to the bottom.

For The Chicken Sauce

Roast the wings and drumsticks until evenly golden in a frying pan, then place in a colander to remove any excess fat.

Caramelise the shallots in a pan, add the tomatoes and cook until they begin to break down. *Deglaze* with the vinegar and reduce until completely evaporated. Transfer all the ingredients, except the butter, to a pressure cooker, cover with water and bring to full pressure. Hold for 20 minutes. Release the steam and strain through a fine sieve. Reduce to desired consistency, then slowly add the butter to *emulsify*. Strain through a fine sieve, set aside.

For The Pomme Purée

Pass the potato flesh through a ricer. Gently add the warm milk, cream and butter to the potatoes until creamy. Pass through a fine sieve and season.

For The Black Garlic Purée

Simmer the ingredients until the water has reduced. Blitz until smooth.

For The Onion Crumb

Preheat the oven to 180°C (fan).

Blend the onion in a food processor with a dash of water until finely chopped. Squeeze out to remove any excess liquid. Bake on a lined tray until dried. Season, then drain on kitchen paper.

For The White Asparagus

Place all the ingredients in a pan. Bring to a simmer, cover with a lid and cook for 15 minutes. Drain, then roast in a hot pan in a splash of oil until browned. Season.

To Serve

Serve as pictured.

LEMON MERINGUE PIE SOUFFLE, HAZELNUT ICE CREAM

SERVES 4

 Frangelico hazelnut liqueur (Italy)
Served on the rocks with a slice of lemon

Ingredients

Hazelnut Ice Cream

600ml whole milk
500g hazelnut paste
150ml double cream
130g caster sugar
90g egg yolk

Lemon Curd

6g agar agar
265ml lemon juice
265g sugar
265g whole egg
375g cold butter (diced)

Soufflé Base

250g caster sugar
125ml water
250ml lemon juice
25g cornflour (mixed to a slurry with a splash of water)

Meringue Crumble Topping

50g hazelnuts
75g egg white
210g caster sugar
120g plain flour
60g butter

Soufflé Mix

200g egg whites
100g caster sugar
200g soufflé base

4 ramekin dishes (buttered, lined with sugar)

Method

For The Hazelnut Ice Cream (Prepare ahead)

Bring the milk, hazelnut paste and cream to the boil.
Whisk the sugar and eggs in a large bowl.
Slowly whisk the warm milk into the eggs. Transfer to a pan and heat to 82°C, then pass through a sieve. Cool, then churn in an ice cream machine. Remove from the freezer 10 minutes before serving.

For The Lemon Curd (Prepare ahead)

Place all the ingredients, except the butter, into a pan and bring to the boil. Whisk thoroughly.
Place the butter into a bowl. Pour the boiling liquid over and stir until smooth. Chill, then blend in a food processor until smooth.

For The Soufflé Base

Place the sugar and water in a pan and bring to 121°C. Add the lemon juice, bring back to the boil, then add the cornflour slurry. Reduce the heat and stir constantly until thickened. Transfer to a bowl and allow to chill.

For The Meringue Crumble Topping

Preheat the oven to 180°C (fan).
Toast the hazelnuts until golden. Leave to cool, then chop.
Whip the egg white in a dry bowl, then add 150g of the sugar. Whisk to firm peaks and place into a piping bag. Pipe mini meringue shells onto a lined baking sheet and bake in the oven until cooked through and dry. Leave to cool, crush into shards.
Combine the remaining sugar and flour in a bowl. Rub in the butter using your fingertips to achieve a breadcrumb consistency. Place onto a baking sheet and bake for 10-15 minutes until golden and crunchy. Leave to cool.
Mix equal quantities of toasted hazelnut, crumble and meringue in a bowl.

For The Soufflé Mix

Preheat the oven to 180°C (fan).
Place the egg whites into a clean bowl and whisk until peaks start to form. Add the sugar and whisk to a meringue consistency. Add the meringue mix to the soufflé base in thirds, until fully combined. Half fill each ramekin with the soufflé mix. Add a tablespoon of lemon curd to each ramekin, then top with the remaining soufflé mix. Smooth off the top with a palette knife to remove any excess mix, then run a thumb around the rim of each mould to create a ridge. Bake in the oven for 8-9 minutes until risen.

To Serve

Top the soufflé with the crumble mixture and serve with hazelnut ice cream.

196
THE WILDERNESS

27 Warstone Lane, Birmingham, B18 6JQ

0121 233 9425
www.wearethewilderness.co.uk Twitter: @thewildernessjq Instagram: @thewildernessjq
Facebook: /thewildernessjq

D on't believe everything you read in the press.

Click-bait pays the bills $$$.

"We're a small, independent restaurant doing whatever the hell we want. We focus on FLAVOUR, above all else; flavour that smacks you in the chops and leaves a lasting treasured memory. We serve modern Birmingham food - a magpie cuisine, borrowing from all the tasty bits of the eclectic melting pot of a city we call home. This restaurant is my love letter to the city - warts and all.

We came from nothing, doing pop-ups in a garden centre and we have not forgotten the journey we took to get where we are today. I rebel against the usual stuffiness that often comes with fine dining and I wanted The Wilderness to be a place in which my old man would feel comfy, in my opinion it should be inclusive luxury, not exclusive. Our food is matched with a classic rock and roll soundtrack, mainly because I have to listen to it 16 hours a day. We offer unusual wines chosen with care and a cocktail/wine flight paired with the food, created by our incredibly talented bar manager.

We've been awarded 3 AA Rosettes and we're Michelin recommended, however this is not traditional fine dining, there are no rules. Led by my brother from another mother and head chef Stuart Deeley, we're working every day to be better, to push the boundaries on modern fine dining and ultimately show you a good time."
Alex Claridge, chef owner.

Rock and roll fine dining - alternative
fine dining focused on flavour and fun.

BIG MAC

SERVES 4

 Adult Appletiser
5ml cognac, 20ml fresh clear apple juice, 20ml
Cà Ed Balos Dorè Passito, 5ml Italicus, 2½ml ice
cider, 2½ml fruit acids, 80ml cava.

Ingredients

Beef Tartare
120g beef bavette (ideally wagyu, ½cm dice)
20g soy caramel, 12g coal oil
8g Maldon salt
20g gherkins (finely diced)
20g shallots (washed, *brunoise*)

Cheddar Custard
100ml double cream
30g Black Bomber extra mature cheddar
52½g pasteurised egg yolks, 1½g salt

Soy Caramel
500ml soy sauce reduced to 250ml
50g caster sugar, 10ml dashi vinegar

Coal Oil
100g burnt coal embers (not hot)
500ml vegetable oil

Gherkin Gel
100g gherkins, 65ml gherkin *liquor*
7g caster sugar, 1½g agar agar

Pickled Shallot Rings
70ml water
100ml white wine vinegar
100g caster sugar, 2g salt
1 banana shallot (finely sliced)

Pickled Shimeji Mushrooms
50ml soy, 12½ml mirin
67½ml rice wine vinegar
15ml sesame oil
1 pack shimeji mushrooms

Chickpea Wafer
250g KTC gram flour, 900ml water
10g rosemary (chopped), 10g salt

Garnish
crispy onions, nasturtiums

Method

For The Beef Tartare
Combine the ingredients.

For The Cheddar Custard
Combine all the ingredients, then cook in a *bain-marie* over a low heat until the custard thickens and coats the back of a wooden spoon.

For The Soy Caramel
Combine the ingredients, then reduce until a *demi-glace* in consistency.

For The Coal Oil (Prepare ahead, will make more than required for this recipe)
Infuse the coal embers in the oil overnight, then strain through a fine muslin cloth.

For The Gherkin Gel
Blend all the ingredients, except the agar agar, then pass through a *chinois*. Add the agar agar and heat to 81°C. Remove from the heat and allow to set. Blend again, then pass through a *chinois*.

For The Pickled Shallot Rings
Combine all the ingredients, except the shallots, and heat until the sugar and salt dissolve. Leave to cool, then add the shallots to the cool *liquor*. Set aside for at least 1 hour.

For The Pickled Shimeji Mushrooms
Combine all the liquids, then add the mushrooms. Set aside for at least 1 hour.

For The Chickpea Wafer (Prepare ahead)
Blend all the ingredients together to form a paste. Spread the paste on greaseproof paper to an even and thin sheet. Freeze overnight. Remove from the freezer and snap into shards. Fry the shards at 180°C until crisp and golden.

To Serve
Serve as pictured.

Chef's Tip
For an easy alternative go to McDonald's and buy a Big Mac.

CHAR SIU PORK, CARROT

SERVES 4

 *Alta Alella Garnatxa Negra, 2018
(Spain)*

Ingredients

Iberico Presa
25g salt, 250ml water
3 white peppercorns
10g thyme, 1 bay leaf
2 star anise, 15g ginger
5g cloves, 200g Iberico presa

Pork Cheek Char Siu/Char Siu Sauce
1 tbsp brown sugar, 20g honey
30g black bean paste, 30ml soy sauce
1 tbsp five spice, 1 tbsp vegetable oil
500ml chicken stock, 1g hot chilli powder
60ml rice wine vinegar
40g smoked pork fat, 2 pork cheeks
panko breadcrumbs (to *pane*)

Glazed Carrots
4 carrots (peeled), 200ml carrot juice
15g unsalted butter, 2g salt, 5 thyme leaves

Manteca
250g *rendered* pork fat
5g rosemary, 1 bay leaf
5g white peppercorns
1 clove garlic

Manteca Crumb
140g panko breadcrumbs, 140g manteca
1½g chilli powder, 2½g salt

Carrot Purée
2 carrots (peeled, chopped), 50g butter, 5g salt
150ml carrot juice, 50ml water

Pickled Carrots
1 carrot (peeled), 50ml white wine vinegar
50g sugar, 37½ml water, 1½g salt

Pak Choi
160g unsalted butter, 500ml water
2g salt, 1g xanthan gum, 1 mini pak choi

Garnish
picked carrot tops

Method

For The Iberico Presa
Combine all the ingredients, except the pork. Add the pork to the brine and leave for 1 hour. Wash off the brine and pat dry with kitchen cloth. Seal the pork in a pan or on a BBQ until the core temperature is 62°C. Rest for 5 minutes.

For The Pork Cheek Char Siu/Char Siu Sauce
Combine all the ingredients, except the pork cheeks, in a pan. Heat the *liquor*, add the cheeks and cook for 1½ hours over a low heat. Remove the cheeks and leave to cool. Reserve the cooking *liquor*.

For The Glazed Carrot
Cook the carrots in a pan with all other ingredients until *al dente*. Remove the carrots, then reduce the *liquor* down to a glaze. To reheat the carrots, do so in a pan with the glaze.

> **Chef's Tip**
>
> Cooking the carrots in their own juice is a fantastic way to ensure a really clean and pure flavour; apply this logic to other root vegetables, such as beetroot, for great results.

For The Manteca
Add all the ingredients to a pan, cook over a low heat for 20 minutes. Remove from the heat and strain the solid ingredients, reserve the fat.

For The Manteca Crumb
Combine all the ingredients.

For The Carrot Purée
Combine all the ingredients in a pan and cook until the carrots are soft. Transfer to a blender and blitz until smooth. Pass through a *chinois*.

For The Pickled Carrots
Finely slice the carrot on a mandoline, then cut into circles using a circle cutter. Combine the remaining ingredients and heat until the sugar dissolves, leave to cool. Reserve the carrot circles in the pickling *liquor* for at least 1 hour.

For The Pak Choi
Combine all the ingredients, except the pak choi, in a pan and bring to a gentle boil. *Blanch* the pak choi in the butter *emulsion* for 1 minute. Do not overcook it.

To Serve
Pane the pork cheek in panko, then deep fry at 180°C until crispy. Serve as pictured.

(see glossary)

MILK & COOKIES

SERVES 4

🍷 *Blandy's 5-Year-Old Malmsey Madeira.*
A delightful bouquet of dried fruit, vanilla and
oak, complementing the underlying cep
mushroom of the course with a toffee note on the
finish to ensure everything about this pairing
indulges the palate.

Ingredients

Cep Caramel

100g caster sugar
50g glucose
50ml water
187½ml double cream
5g cep powder

Cep Cookie

47½g soft, light brown sugar
47½g unsalted butter
25g condensed milk
3¾g cep powder
25g milk chocolate (chopped)
65g plain flour
3¾g baking powder

Salted Milk Ice Cream

600ml whole milk
100g glucose
80g caster sugar
15g vanilla extract
12½g salt
4g gellan gum
2½g silk gel texture improver

Method

For The Cep Caramel

Caramelise the sugar, glucose and water in a pan over a medium heat until golden brown. Add the cream and whisk in the cep powder. Pass through a sieve.

For The Cep Cookie

Cream the butter and sugar in a stand mixer. Add the remaining ingredients and bring together as a dough. Roll into a ballotine and chill.

Preheat the oven to 180°C (fan).

Cut the cookies as required and bake for 5 minutes.

> **Chef's Tip**
>
> Don't discount mushroom as a great dessert ingredient –
> we use it to bring complexity and umami notes to desserts.
> It's a great flavour friend to chocolate. Experiment!

For The Salted Milk Ice Cream

Combine all the ingredients in a pan. Heat to 82°C, then remove from the heat and blend. Churn in an ice cream machine.

To Serve

Serve as pictured.

207

M&J SMETHWICK
A proper, no-nonsense fishmonger

It goes without saying that to have exceptional ingredients at the heart of your menu, you need suppliers who are true specialists in their fields. And, when it comes to looking for the highest quality fish and seafood, you need a proper, no-nonsense fishmonger.

You'll want a fishmonger who's local but has access to all the UK markets, who can bring you the finest examples of seasonally caught British fish and seafood, as well as the best of the world's catch.

What's more, you would never want them to damage your reputation by selling you fish that is endangered or on the Marine Conservation Society's (MCS) fish to avoid list. You'll want a fishmonger who has the knowledge and skill to prepare it how you like it and deliver it safely to your kitchen door, as fresh as the hour it was caught.

M&J does all this, and more. They first started selling fish and seafood over 40 years ago and since then, have opened branches across Britain supplying chefs in the local area.

M&J Smethwick, like every other M&J branch, are their own entity. They buy their own fish and seafood based on what's been landed each morning and what's needed by their customers, which include many Midland-based Michelin star and AA Rosette restaurants.

They can get pretty much anything you're looking for, providing of course, it is in season and sustainably caught or farmed. This includes a range of provenance-rich British fish and seafood, caught by skippers on day-boats around the UK coast.

Alongside their own telesales team and buyers, M&J Smethwick also has their own team of fishmongers.

Fishmongers are at the heart of M&J. Their knowledge and craft is handed down through generations. And, with a combined experience of over 161 years, the team at M&J Smethwick have some of the best fishmongers in the business. Their ranks include three winners of the National Federation of Fishmongers' British Fish Craft Championships. One of these is Dave Bennett, who also holds the coveted title Master Fishmonger. Together, they're responsible for making sure the standard of fish and seafood, and the quality of the prep, is nothing less than, well... award-winning.

Like your business, M&J Smethwick is non stop. They're buying fish from the moment the markets open at dawn and prepare the catch overnight. It's a 24-hour, 6 day a week operation, which means even if you place an order after evening service, you could still get a delivery the next morning.

You won't get fresher than that now, will you?

For more information, give M&J Smethwick a call on 0121 565 6270.
M&J Smethwick, Potterton Way, Smethwick, B66 1AU www.mjseafood.com

208
RELISH MIDLANDS LARDER

FISH

KINGFISHER MIDLANDS
Austin Way, Great Barr, Birmingham, B42 1DU.
T: 0121 6228 830 www.kingfishermidlands.co.uk
*Experienced fishmongers supplying quality fresh fish
and seafood to the catering industry throughout the
Midlands. They source, prepare and deliver fresh and
frozen fish and seafood directly to professional
kitchens. Suppliers to all types of catering
establishments from Michelin-starred restaurants,
hotels, pubs, retail outlets, schools, colleges and
universities to sports stadiums and contract caterers.*

*They have links with fishing ports around the UK
enabling them to buy fresh from local day fishing
boats. They also have strong links with overseas
suppliers allowing them to offer a great variety of
fish and seafood.*

M&J SMETHWICK
Potterton Way, Smethwick, B66 1AU.
T: 0121 565 6270 www.mjseafood.com
M&J Smethwick *first started selling fish and
seafood over 40 years ago and since then, have
opened branches across Britain supplying chefs in
the local area.*

*M&J Smethwick, like every other M&J branch, are
their own entity. They buy their own fish and
seafood based on what's been landed each morning
and what's needed by their customers, which
include many Midland-based Michelin star and
AA Rosette restaurants.*

*They can get pretty much anything you're looking
for, providing of course, it is in season and
sustainably caught or farmed.*

MEAT

AUBREY ALLEN, BUTCHER & DELICATESSEN
108 Warwick Street, Leamington Spa,
Warwickshire, CV32 4QP.
T: 01926 311 208 www.aubreyallenleamington.co.uk
*This family business opened over 80 years ago,
started by the orphan Aubrey Allen as a small, back
street butcher's shop in Coventry. The company has
evolved over the years to what it is today - one of
the best-known butchers in the Midlands and
throughout the UK. They have grown through their
commitment to making the best quality meat
available to their customers and were recently
awarded Delicatessen of the Year at the Guild of
Fine Food.*

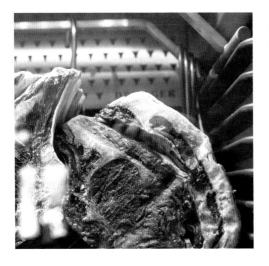

KNIGHTWICK BUTCHERS
Bromyard Road, Knightwick, Worcester,
Worcestershire, WR6 5PH.
T: 01886 821 585 www.knightwickbutchers.com
*Suppliers of quality meat to trade and
non-trade customers.*

THE SHROPSHIRE BOAR COMPANY
T: 07543 282 382
www.theshropshireboarcompany.co.uk
Suppliers of pure bred wild boar meat.

210
RELISH MIDLANDS LARDER

FRUIT & VEGETABLES

AUGERNIK FRUIT FARM
Hopton Wafers, Shropshire, DY14 0HH.
T: 01299 272 870 www.augernikfruitfarm.weebly.com
*An independent fruit farm growing naturally since
1989, proudly owned by the Auger family.*

NEIL FRANCE QUALITY FRUIT & VEGETABLES
Unit 7, Aston Road Business Park, Wem,
Shropshire, SY4 5BA.
T: 01939 235 531
*Quality fruit and vegetables delivered direct to
trade. With over seven years' experience in the
industry, Neil France delivers the highest possible
standard of produce at very competitive prices.*

FINE & SPECIALITY FOODS

BENNETT & DUNN RAPESEED OIL
Bridgnorth, Shropshire.
T: 07474 887 453 www.bennettanddunn.co.uk
*Bennett & Dunn cold pressed rapeseed oil is
produced by husband and wife team Rupert and
Tracey Bennett. Rupert takes great pride in
producing a superior quality product.
The rapeseed is cold pressed, triple filtered, then
hand bottled by Rupert on the farm. The oil is GM
free, gluten free and the production process is
chemical free, ensuring the rapeseed oil retains all
its health benefits and delicious flavour. It's full of
natural goodness.*

HARVEY & BROCKLESS (THE FINE FOOD COMPANY)

Broomhall Farm, Broomhall, Worcester, WR5 2NT.
T: 01905 829 830 www.harveyandbrockless.co.uk
Producers and distributors of speciality foods, working with artisan food producers across the globe.

ROWLANDS & CO (SHREWSBURY) LTD

Knights Way, Battlefield Enterprise Park, Shrewsbury, SY1 3AB.
T: 01743 462 244 www.rowlandsltd.co.uk
A family owned business, offering the best quality fresh produce at a competitive price to the catering trade since 1894.

FARM SHOPS

HARE HILL FARM

Edgton, Shropshire.
T: 07896 413 894 www.harehillfarm.co.uk
Providing local communities and restaurants with seasonal, fresh produce.

212
RELISH MIDLANDS LARDER

LUDLOW FARM SHOP
Bromfield, Ludlow, Shropshire, SY8 2JR.
T: 01584 856 000 www.ludlowfarmshop.co.uk
*Ludlow Farm Shop, is the new name for Ludlow Food
Centre. They produce over half of the products that
they sell on site. In fact, they have looked to open
more windows into the production areas so that you
can see your food being made.*

*Ludlow Farm Shop is a one-of-a-kind food shopping
experience where farming, food production and
retailing come together to create an award-winning
environment. They are part of the Earl of Plymouth's
Oakly Park Estate which extends to approximately
8,000 acres of Shropshire countryside of which they
farm in hand 6,500 acres. All of their beef, lamb and
Gloucester Old Spot pork comes from their farm
along with the milk used to make our cheese and
dairy products. They have a herd of wild fallow deer
roaming the estate and a bountiful supply of wild
game at certain times of the year.*

CHEESE & DAIRY

MAWLEY MILK
Mawley Town Farm, Cleobury Mortimer, DY14 8PJ.
T: 01299 270 359 www.mawleytownfarm.co.uk
*With high animal welfare and being
environmentally sustainable, Mawley Town Farm
offers some of the best Shropshire milk and cream.*

MOYDENS HANDMADE CHEESE
The Creamery, Lockley Villa Farm
Wistanswick, Market Drayton, TF9 2AY.
T: 01630 639 796 www.moydenscheese.co.uk
*Established in 2005 by Martin Moyden, Mr Moyden's
Handmade Cheese has fast become a well-respected
artisan cheesemaking business. This stems from a
passion for quality, attention to detail and a lust
for perfection.*

ASTLEY
VINEYARD

Established in 1971, Astley Vineyard is one of the oldest vineyards in the UK. Tucked away in the River Severn valley, the family owned business produces a range of award-winning white wines in its own winery.

The vineyard's stylish new cellar door shop is separated by a wooded valley from a pretty five acre vineyard. Whether you would like to buy one bottle or a case, join a tour or organise a private event, get in touch. Shop open weekends only.

ASTLEY VINEYARD | Boutique Worcestershire Wine
Hampstall Lane, Stourport on Severn, DY13 0RU
www.astleyvineyard.co.uk T: 01299 822 907

BEVERAGES

PURITY BREWING CO
The Brewery, Upper Spernall Farm, Off Spernal Lane, Great Alne, Warwickshire, B49 6JF.
T: 01789 488 007 www.puritybrewing.com
When Purity Brewing Company set out the mission was simple: brew great beer without prejudice, with a conscience and with a consistency and an attention to detail, which is second to none. The number of awards they've won both on a national and international stage is a true testament to the quality, skill and dedication of the whole Purity team.

SMOKED FOOD

MACNEIL'S SMOKEHOUSE
Rushock Trading Estate, 338, Rushock, Droitwich, WR9 0NR.
T: 01299 253 764 www.macneilssmokehouse.co.uk
Macneil's Smokehouse is a family run, artisan producer in Worcestershire producing the finest smoked products for retailers and caterers.

215
WINE PAIRING BY ADAM STOKES

"At Adam's we work on food and wine matching in two different ways; flavour marriages and flavour contrasts. The marriage approach is matching similar flavours, finding a harmony between flavours and textures on the plate and in the glass. Also trying to match the weight of the food and the wine, for example, a rich beef dish with truffles can be paired with a full-bodied, aged red wine from Pomerol.

The contrasts approach is about finding wines and food at opposite ends of the flavour spectrum. The key is to strike a balance of flavour intensity and texture through their interaction. An example of this is to match a zesty young Sancerre with cod fillet in a rich mussel and Champagne sauce.

One of my top tips is not to worry too much about the colour of the wine with the food. Light-bodied, chilled red wines work well with big fish dishes and a big Montrachet would really complement a chicken or pork dish. I find that each wine is unique and, regardless of the grape variety and region, each vintage has its own character. The difference between a red Bordeaux from 2007 (a very poor year) to a 2009 vintage (a great year) has dramatic differences in the flavour, not to mention the cost of the 2007 is nearly half of 2009 for most Château.

The developed flavour of aged vintage Champagnes are fabulous to match with food - even desserts, when the honey flavours are being released from the Champagne with toasty and nutty flavours coming through.

On a personal level, there is really no right or wrong when it comes to matching wine to food, it is better to drink things that you enjoy, and many wines go very well with lots of foods. Matching wine and food adds layers and complexity which can make a tasting menu more enjoyable."

Adam Stokes
Chef Patron, Adam's

AL DENTE
Al dente describes vegetables that are cooked to the 'tender crisp' phase - still offering resistance to the bite, but cooked through. Al dente can also describe cooked pasta which is firm but not hard.

BAIN-MARIE
A pan or other container of hot water with a bowl placed on top of it. This allows the steam from the water to heat the bowl so ingredients can be gently heated or melted.

BEURRE NOISETTE
Unsalted butter is melted over a low heat until it begins to caramelise and brown. When it turns a nutty colour, it should be removed from the heat to stop it burning. Can be used as a base for butter sauces or added to cakes and batters.

BLANCH
Boiling an ingredient before removing it and plunging it in ice cold water in order to stop the cooking process.

BRUNOISE
A type of culinary cut in which food is diced into quarter inch (3.175mm) cubes. The formal-looking little squares add colour and elegance to dishes.

CARTOUCHE
A piece of greaseproof paper that covers the surface of a stew, soup, stock or sauce to reduce evaporation.

CHINOIS
A conical sieve with an extremely fine mesh. It is used to strain custards, purées, soups and sauces, producing a very smooth texture.

CLARIFIED BUTTER
Milk fat rendered from butter to separate the milk solids and water from the butter fat.

CONCASSE
To roughly chop any ingredient, usually vegetables, most specifically applied to tomatoes, with tomato concasse being a tomato that has been peeled and seeded (seeds and skin removed).

CONFIT
A method of cooking where the meat is cooked and submerged in a liquid to add flavour. Often this liquid is rendered fat. Confit can also apply to fruits - fruit confits are cooked and preserved in sugar, the result is like candied fruits.

DEGLAZE
To make a gravy or sauce by adding liquid to the cooking juices and food particles in a pan in which meat or other ingredients have been cooked.

DEMI-GLACE
A rich brown sauce in French cuisine used by itself or as a base for other sauces.

EMULSION/EMULSIFY
In the culinary arts, an emulsion is a mixture of two liquids that would ordinarily not mix together, like oil and vinegar.

FRENCH TRIM
Fat, meat or skin is cut away to expose a piece of bone, so that it sticks out. It also means that any excess fat is cut off. French Trimming can be done to lamb chops and bigger cuts; it can even can be done to chicken legs or breasts.

JULIENNE
A culinary knife cut in which the vegetable is sliced into long thin strips, similar to matchsticks.

LARDER TRIMMED
The term given to steaks which have been trimmed to leave only the eye of the steak. This cut is often used in a beef Wellington.

LIQUOR
The liquid that is left over from the cooking of meat or vegetables. Can be incorporated into sauces and gravy.

MACERATE/MACERATED
Raw, dried or preserved fruit and vegetables soaked in a liquid to soften the food or to absorb the flavour.

MIREPOIX
Finely diced combination of celery (pascal, celery or celeriac), onions and carrots. There are many regional mirepoix variations, which can sometimes be just one of these ingredients, or include additional spices creating a rich, flavoursome base to sauces or stews.

PANE
To coat with flour, beaten egg and breadcrumbs for deep frying.

QUENELLE
A neat, three-sided oval (resembling a mini rugby ball) that is formed by gently smoothing the mixture between two dessertspoons.

RENDER
To render is to melt and clarify hard animal fat in dry heat or wet heat.

ROCHER
A one-handed quenelle.

SABAYON
Made by beating egg yolks with a liquid over simmering water until thickened and increased in volume. The liquid can be water, but Champagne or wine is often used.

SAUTE
To fry in a small amount of fat.

SOUS VIDE
French for 'under vacuum.' A method of cooking food sealed in airtight plastic bags in a water bath or in a temperature-controlled steam environment for longer than normal cooking times. The intention is to cook the item evenly, ensuring that the inside is properly cooked without overcooking the outside, and to retain moisture.

TEMPER
To temper eggs is to add a hot liquid to an egg mixture without cooking the eggs. Tempering is to slowly bring up the temperature of the eggs without scrambling them. Tempering also refers to a process of heating and cooling chocolate to prepare it for dipping and enrobing. The tempering process ensures a smooth texture, a glossy shine and a pleasant 'snap' when bitten or broken.

ALL THE INGREDIENTS FOR YOUR RECIPE TO SUCCESS

Relish is proud to have worked with more than 1500 of the UK's best-loved chefs to showcase their wonderful restaurants and food but there is a huge appetite for more.

Paul Askew, Mark Greenaway, Jean Christophe Novelli and Dipna Anand are just four of the industry's leading lights who worked with our small, professional and dedicated team to produce their own beautiful books - stamped with their personality and signature dishes.

Mark's book Perceptions was named the world's best chef cookbook at the Gourmand World Cookbook Awards. It is an amazing accolade and testament to Mark's passion for the art and the wonderful natural larder he works with. Perceptions is an outstanding example of how, as an independent publisher, we are able to focus on you, your restaurant and your region to showcase culinary excellence to our readers who are always hungry to try out new dishes.

Owning this book is just for starters, reading it is the main course. Why not go for dessert and let us help you create a bespoke publication of your own to share with your loyal customers and attract new fans along the way? You will be on the shelves alongside our fantastic portfolio of beautifully illustrated guides, which are stocked nationally in Waterstones, Harvey Nichols, in each featured restaurant, in leading independent stores and online globally. You could be the next published chef to join the world's elite.

Relish has a small, friendly, professional team, with experience in publishing, print management, editing, proofing, photography, design and artwork, sales distribution and marketing. We ensure a personal approach, working exceptionally hard to develop a great product which reflects each chef's talent and passion.

Duncan and Teresa Peters established the company in 2009, with a vision of building a niche publishing house for food lovers. The success of Relish Publications is reflected in the fact that we are the UK's leading regional recipe book publisher.

For more information contact our friendly, dedicated team at marketing@relishpublications.co.uk

"Relish books are full of enjoyable recipes and ideas for making the most of the edible treasures we have on our doorstep; both places to eat them and new, exciting ways to cook them."

Angela Hartnett, MBE

"The Relish cookbook offers the home cook some great inspiration to make the most of these wonderful ingredients in season."

Tom Kitchin

"With mouthwatering, easy to follow recipes and beautiful photography, Relish South West is a must have for any foodie, from professional chef to the inspired home cook."

Michael Caines MBE

"Relish North East & Yorkshire showcases some extremely hardworking chefs. Enjoy their recipes and the inspiration behind them but, best of all, go and discover their restaurants, taste what they do and experience some great northern hospitality."

Michael Wignall

"Relish Midlands is a fantastic recipe book that brings together so many of the talented chefs and quality restaurants in the area. It gives you a taste of what our exciting region has to offer as well as the encouragement to try some new recipes."

Adam Stokes

"Relish Wales is a fabulous way to showcase some of our beautiful country's fabulous eateries and to be able to share our food with a wider audience."

Stephen Terry

AVAILABLE TO BUY IN OUR FEATURED RESTAURANTS & IN ALL GOOD BOOKSHOPS

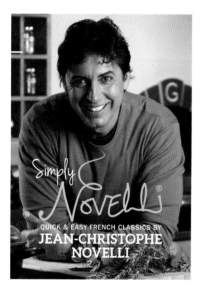

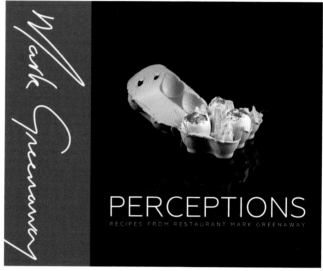

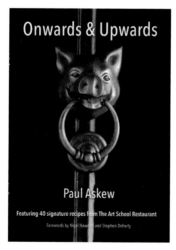

Relish
SCOTLAND
FOURTH EDITION

Original recipes from Scotland's finest chefs and restaurants. Introduction by chef Geoffrey Smeddle.

Relish
SOUTH WEST

Original recipes from the South West's finest chefs and restaurants. Introduction by Michael Caines MBE.

Relish
NORTH EAST & YORKSHIRE
THIRD EDITION

Original recipes from the regions' best-loved chefs and restaurants. Introduction by chef patron Michael Wignall.

Relish
NORTH WEST
SECOND HELPING

Original recipes from the region's finest chefs and restaurants. Introduction by chef Paul Askew.

Relish
MIDLANDS
THIRD EDITION

Original recipes from the region's best-loved chefs and restaurants. Introduction by chef patron Glynn Purnell.

Relish
WALES
THIRD EDITION

Original recipes from the region's finest chefs and restaurants. Introduction by chef Will Holland.

HOW TO MAKE ICE CREAM WITHOUT A MACHINE

Although relatively inexpensive these days, not everyone has access to an ice cream machine. That's no reason not to follow some of these delicious recipes found in the Relish Midlands book. Although more time consuming than a machine, excellent results can be obtained by following this simple method.

Follow the recipe right up until it tells you to churn in the machine, including any chilling time in the fridge.

Take your mixture from the fridge and stir with a rubber spatula. Transfer it to a suitable plastic container with a lid. There should be at least 2cm space at the top to allow the mixture to expand when freezing. Cover and place in the freezer for two hours.

Remove from the freezer and beat with a hand mixer, still in the container, to break up the ice crystals that are beginning to form. Cover and return to the freezer for a further 2 hours. (If you don't have a hand mixer then you may use a fork and some 'elbow grease' to break up the crystals).

Remove from the freezer and beat again with the hand mixer. The ice cream should be thickening up nicely at this point but too soft to scoop. Return it to the freezer for an additional hour. Beat again. If your ice cream is still not thickened sufficiently, repeat this process again after another hour. When the ice cream has thickened properly, stir in any add-ins at this point (honeycomb, nuts...). Do not beat with the hand mixer after the add-ins have been mixed in.

Place the tightly sealed container in the freezer and allow the ice cream to freeze until firm. The ice cream should be removed from the freezer 15-20 minutes before you wish to eat it. This will make scooping easier.

This method will also work for sorbets. Sometimes sorbets may go a bit 'icy' or 'crumbly' if left for too long in the freezer. This can be rectified by blitzing in a food processor just before serving.

Lemon Meringue Pie Soufflé, Hazelnut Ice Cream - **Page 194**

HOW TO MAKE A SUGAR STOCK SYRUP

This makes about 750ml sugar stock. It can be stored in a sterilised jar in the fridge for a couple of months.

500g white sugar
500ml water

Place the sugar and water in a pan. Dissolve slowly over a very low heat. You must not allow the syrup to boil until all the sugar has dissolved, about 5 minutes. Once completely dissolved, bring to the boil, then simmer for 5 minutes.

CONVERSION CHART

TEMPERATURE CONVERSIONS

To convert Fahrenheit to Celsius, subtract 32, multiply by 5, then divide by 9. To convert Celsius to Fahrenheit, multiply by 9, divide by 5, then add 32. See the table below for some common temperature equivalents used in cooking.

Description	Fahrenheit	Celsius	Gas Mark
Room Temperature	68 F to 72 F	20 C to 22 C	
Poach Temperature	160 F to 180 F	70 C to 82 C	
Simmer Temperature	185 F to 205 F	85 C to 95 C	
Boil Temperature	212 F	100 C	
Very Cool Oven	225 F	110 C	1/4
Cool Oven	250 F	120 C	1/2
Low Oven	325 F	160 C	3
Moderate Oven	350 F	180 C	4
Hot Oven	400 F to 425 F	200 C to 220 C	6 to 7

*Temperatures for fan-assisted ovens are, as a general rule, normally about 20°C lower than regular oven temperatures.

WEIGHT MEASUREMENT CONVERSIONS

1 teaspoon (5ml/5g)	$^1/_4$ oz
1 tablespoon (15ml/15g)	$^3/_4$ oz
10g	$^1/_2$ oz
25g	1oz
50g	2oz
75g	3oz
150g	5oz
200g	7oz
250g	9oz
350g	12oz
450g	1lb
1kg	2.2lb

VOLUME MEASUREMENT CONVERSIONS

55ml	2 fl oz
150ml	$^1/_4$ pt
275ml	$^1/_2$ pt
570ml	1 pt
1 litre	$1^3/_4$ pt

Note: All oven temperatures in this book are for non fan ovens unless otherwise stated.

These are approximate conversions, which have been either rounded up or down.

When following a recipe, never mix metric and imperial measures. Stick to one or the other.